THE OLD PRO TURKEY HUNTER

by

Gene Nunnery

A   PORTALS   BOOK

ISBN 0-916620-48-4

LIBRARY OF CONGRESS CARD CATALOG NO. 80-80630

MANUFACTURED IN THE UNITED STATES OF AMERICA

Contents

My deep gratitude to Mr. Norman C. Miller, Jr. of Camden, Alabama for his outstanding artwork for my book. The beautiful full color painting and all the pen-and-ink portrayals were created specially for this book by Mr. Miller.

Mr. Miller is a lover of the wild turkey and this love shows in every stroke of his brush and pen. His long days afield studying and hunting the wild turkey have inspired him to capture, on canvas, and on paper, the true look and mood of his elusive subject.

I covet the ability to portray the wild turkey in writing with the same degree of genius as Mr. Miller's artworks so ably do. Thanks Norman, you are truly a turkey man.

GENE NUNNERY

Foreword

PEOPLE who read this book may have in mind that hidden in its pages may be a magic formula for killing a wild turkey. While it is probably true that any turkey hunter, young or old, will be a better turkey hunter after reading it, it could also be true, that even if the reader will learn to be a better turkey hunter, he may, in fact, actually kill fewer turkeys. How can this be? The fact is the old pro turkey hunters who march through the pages of this book are going to convince you that real turkey hunting doesn't always necessarily have to include a pile of feathers and blood. These old master turkey hunters hunted wild turkeys without having to abide by hunting seasons, bag limits, game wardens, or any other restrictions. They found that the real reward for successful turkey hunting lay in winning the battle, not necessarily exterminating the foe.

This book may help you become a master turkey hunter. It may help you become sure enough of your ability as a turkey hunter so you can, at times, call up a magnificent turkey gobbler and, when his life is in your hands, let him live. When you let a gobbler walk away from you, don't expect people to understand. In the first place, few people understand what it is about turkey hunting that makes a person get out of a warm bed at three o'clock on a cold spring morning and take on unbelievable obstacles before reaching his "turkey place."

Thus this book is written as a message to the wild turkey hunters of America. We hope it will serve as a bond between the old pro turkey hunter of the past and the 'now generation' of turkey hunters. The book deals with four old pro turkey hunters who spent over two hundred years trying to figure out the complex nature of the wild turkey. What a waste it would be to let slip from us the hard-gained knowledge they acquired.

At this point I want to present my credentials. I am sixty-eight years old and have hunted wild turkeys every single year for the last fifty-three. I have killed 248 gobblers during the fifty-three years. The breakdown is as follows:

My first   10 years to hunt, average 2 per year - 2 x 10 = 20
My second 10 years to hunt, average 3 per year - 3 x 10 = 30
My third   10 years to hunt, average 5 per year - 5 x 10 = 50
My fourth 10 years to hunt, average 7 per year - 7 x 10 = 70
My past   13 years to hunt, average 6 per year - 6 x 14 = 78

    53 years to hunt, total turkeys killed   248

    These turkeys were killed chiefly in Alabama and Mississippi. All turkeys were killed in season and within the legal bag limits. For the last twenty years I have set my own bag limit well below the legal limits of the states in which I hunt wild turkeys. I humbly submit these facts and figures to you in an attempt to convince you that I am a "turkey man" and an "old pro."

    This brings me to the point of asking you as a reader to accept as true the many astounding acts and maneuvers of the turkey gobblers I called and observed over all these years. As you yourself hunt the wild turkey, some, if not all, of the amazing accounts of wild turkey's behavior related in this book will be verified by the turkeys themselves. What other activity of man exists that could so fascinate a man that, even after a half century of indulgence, he looks forward to each turkey season with childlike enthusiasm? As old age creeps up on a turkey hunter, his eyesight will dim, his hearing fade, his activities diminish, and his desires lessen, but as long as a wild turkey gobbler is out there to be hunted, somehow the old man is going to get to him. That's for sure.

    Today the National Wild Turkey Federation is putting on the greatest calling contest of all time. This fine organization is calling together all the hunters, observers, and lovers of the wild turkey. The Federation would have us join hands to continue one of the most remarkable natural phenomena of this century, the comeback of the wild turkey. We believe you should join this fine organization: The National Wild Turkey Federation, P. O. Box 467, Edgefield, S.C. 29824.

    Perhaps it would have been appropriate to have named this book, "How to Kill Fewer Wild Turkeys and Enjoy It More."

                                                    G. N.

I am Jack Dudley—1969 National Champion, 1971 King of Champions, and 1977 King of Champions Turkey Caller. I started hunting wild turkeys when I was seventeen years old. I have been hunting them for twenty-three years. I have killed lots of wild turkeys. This book that you are about to read is the best I have ever read on the true facts and the tales of old turkey hunters. This knowledge of the wild turkey and the knowledge of the turkey hunter, young and old, was not gained by hearsay. It was gained by experience alone. Gene Nunnery has experienced so many times the art of winning the battle with the great wild turkey and the agony of defeat. All of us that have turkey-hunted know what this means. There is nothing equal to hunting the king of the woods and hunting him like this book tells you, one on one. Any one can learn to call and handle a wild turkey using the methods that are told in this book. This man is truly from the old school. He is one of the most dedicated turkey hunters of our time. Thanks, Mr. Gene, for people like you. I hope I can last thirty more years.

JACK L. DUDLEY
Dekalb, Mississippi

The Old Pro Turkey Hunter is one of the best books I have ever read on the greatest of all sports, how to hunt the old gobbler. What makes any story about hunting is the memory of each hunt. The Old Pro, Gene Nunnery, has a thousand memories and in this book he shares them with us all. As you know, each turkey is an individual itself, and through this book you can learn how to judge each turkey and each experience. What helped make me the turkey hunter and caller that I am was sitting around and listening to all the old turkey hunters tell of their experiences. This book of old turkey stories will make you a better turkey hunter. It is written for the old turkey hunters and the new. It will help you become a Master in the Greatest sport, Hunting and Calling the Elusive Gobbler.

BEN RODGERS LEE
Coffeeville, Alabama

Hope you will find some old gobblers, battle worn and wise, to challenge you.

1

Gabe Meadow

I HAVE sometimes heard of persons with a liking for gambling who make a killing and are forever after handicapped by the instant success. The lucky gambler thrusts himself into the grinding mill of chance, trying to repeat the feat. Over fifty years ago, Lady Luck annointed this writer with fabulous success in a duel of life and death with a wild turkey gobbler. So here I am, barefaced, aged, humble, and disciplined trying to share with you the time in between—a span of half a century and a life almost spent trying to become the master of the wild turkey.

I think the nearest I came to reaching my goal was over fifty years ago during my first year to hunt the wild turkey. As a country boy in his teens, I was a good outdoorsman. I knew the ways of the creatures of the woods and its streams. I heard tales told of the wild turkey by the few men who hunted them. The turkey hunters were in a class by themselves. They looked different, acted different, and I found out, were different. They usually, I always thought, looked hungry. They had so little in common with other hunters that seldom did I see them talking to the fox hunters or the bird (quail) hunters or other hunters. The man I shined up to for the purpose of learning about turkeys was about the most rabid of the lot. He was pretty helpful during the first Fall and Winter of our association; but even during this first year, as the spring gobbling season approached, he became moody, crabby, and, at times, downright mean. He seemed to sense I would take all his moods in stride. He was correct for he had in his possession the knowledge I was hellbent to come by. We made a strange combination; a teen-age boy and a man in his late sixties.

Gabe Meadow was one of the best all-round hunters I have ever seen and his specialty was the wild turkey. I believe very few turkey hunters attain the rank of "Master Turkey Hunter" and Gabe was truly a master of the art. He was well equipped. Lean and lithe and with a natural curiosity to find out everything in nature. All his spare time was spent roaming the fields and forests. He was the only man I ever knew who could follow a drove of wild turkeys all day long from morning flydown to afternoon flyup. I have seen him, after one of these days of following a flock, sit down as relaxed and as happy as a man could be. He would detail the events of the day: the frequent spooking of the flock by unexplained noises and movements, the many moods of the turkeys happily hopping around at times, the many mock fights, and the constant serious mood of one or two old hens of the flock who disapproved of the frolicking of the others.

I had a feeling that in his own good time Gabe would share with me some of his turkey hunting secrets. I was correct. During a warm sunny break in the weather on a February day, Gabe and I were walking an old logging road when he suddenly stopped. By the road stood a very large beautiful beech tree. Gabe walked up to it and patted its smooth trunk and said, "Indian Umbrella." Gabe said the Indians used the beech for shelter during rainstorms because lightning didn't strike beech trees. Now how or why I don't know, but in the fifty years after hearing this I haven't seen or heard of anyone who has ever seen a beech tree that has been struck by lightning.

Gabe sat down in front of this beech and leaned back against its trunk. Then it came: How to kill a wild turkey. Gabe's technique was really quite simple. For over fifty years I have gone over his plans word by word and move by move. Many times I have departed from his advice as I sought better ways, wanting always to invent my own foolproof methods. A foolproof way to kill a wild turkey, I now realize, just doesn't exist and you don't want it. The uncertainty of the hunt is a fascination of the sport.

Gabe laid it out. The best way to make a turkey gobble is to owl. This is the act of imitating the owl in turkey territory. Start owling at the first light of day; keep it up in series of hoots until he gobbles. Many times as you hoot, real owls will come up and you can let them take over. There are many theories as to why a gobbler will sound off at the owl's hoot. Some say the owl is the turkey's enemy. Gabe said this ain't so. The reason he gobbles at the owl is quite simple. It's the spirit of competition. The vain, egotistical gobbler thinks his gobble is the most wonderful sound of the forest. When he hears a distinct sound like an owl hoot rise above the melody of the forest, he simply wants to cap it off with his own wonderful gobble. Often he will gobble at any distinct sound that rises above the din of forest sounds: the whistle of the red bird, a crow's caw, a sharp clap of thunder, a train whistle, the slamming of a car door, even the distant boom of a gun.

Gabe continued to lay it out. After you locate your gobbler, move quickly and quietly to within one-hundred to one-hundred fifty yards of him. (The distance would depend on the terrain cover, and amount of light.) Find a tree about the size of your body and without bushes and briars close to its base. Don't try to hide in thickets. Don't get behind trees, stumps, etc. You want to be in front of them. When you get this close to a wild turkey gobbler, every move and decision you make will bear heavily on the outcome of the pending fray. One mistake of move or judgment and it's all over.

The reason you elect to sit in front of the tree is quite simple. You can see the turkey before he sees you—a very important fact in your favor. Now you are sitting flat on the ground slumped down to where your caboose is about six inches from the base of the tree. The vest with the game pocket in back is packed with rain gear, extra clothes, etc., and it supports the small of your back as you sit. Your knees are pulled up in front of you, your gun rests between your knees, your cap is pulled down. Now you are looking through a small opening between the bill of your cap and the top of your knees. Your face is completely hidden.

You don't have to have a wild gobbler out there scaring the hell out of you to practice this tree-sitting technique. Fact is, you'd be much better off doing the practicing in your front yard. Learn how to sit with the least amount of discomfort. Sit for minutes in the beginning, then for an hour or more as you progress. If you shoot from your right shoulder, you should sit facing slightly to the right of where your turkey is located. Once you work out this tree-sitting technique, you should be able to sit for hours, gun resting on your knees. If your turkey circles to approach from another direction, you move around the base of the tree, always facing in his general direction.

As already said, I didn't just accept Gabe's advice as the iron-clad, unbending "way you do it." Fact is I guess in my early years I kind of resented it being laid out so nice and pat. So I tried every other possible way to confront a wild turkey. I climbed trees. (One day your age will take care of the temptation to this.) I lay down. I hid in thickets. I stood behind trees and stumps and brush piles. I even dug several holes in turkey-gobbling territory so I could get in one to call my turkey. Let me say here, the "get in hole" technique is the worst possible way and the next worst is to lie down. Once during my hole diggin' days, I had two gobblers pin me down in my hole for two and one half hours. To this day I believe these gobblers knew the score and deliberately kept me confined in my semi-grave to their great satisfaction. Never before or since have I heard the going on that these two gobblers let out. They gobbled. They drummed. They strutted. They clucked. They paraded, as they played the game I invented named "sucker in the hole." Never once did I see them.

Gabe had made a small box call for me. It was about six inches long, about one inch thick, and hollow. One side had a lid extending about 3/8 of an inch. The call was held in one hand and scraped on a piece of slate held in the other hand. I am sure it wouldn't win any turkey calling contests, but over the fifty years I have owned it, it has won the hearts of many trophy gobblers. Gabe showed me how to use it and advised me to practice with it until I could use it with confidence. Gabe was an advocate of very little yelping. He would say, "If you like to yelp and get a kick out of it, that's fine. But don't do it around a turkey gobbler." Three to five soft rapid ke-uk ke-uk ke-uk ke-uk ke-uk's was all he laid on a gobbler. That, he said, was the true mating call of the wild turkey hen. Real love talk. Why mess it up with all kinds of other sounds when this is what sends the fire rushing to Mr. Gobbler's head, lighting up his wattles with crimson, and drenching his brain with desire. After you have made the call, put your caller up so you won't be tempted to keep yelping with it.

There is no better time than now to give you one of Gabe's favorite sayings, "Always expect the unexpected when dealing with a wild turkey." I believe Gabe could have talked for a month explaining this and proving it with some of the soundest logic you ever heard.

The spring turkey season was almost at hand, and I felt prepared to launch my turkey hunting career. Over fifty years ago it happened and I remember it as if it were yesterday. I knew the place this bunch of turkeys used since I had watched them for hours on end and days at a time. Fact is, I had tried to waylay an old gobbler who was frequently seen with the bunch. He seemed to lead a charmed life, for he never came in range of my single-barrel twenty-gauge.

Gabe would simply have gone into orbit had he known of such a nefarious attempt on the life of that gobbler. I sensed this early in my association with Gabe. As our friendship grew over the years, so did my respect for Gabe's unbending rules for hunting the wild turkey. To retain the unique challenge of real wild turkey hunting you have to be willing to give the turkey a sporting chance. Given this chance, a wise old gobbler can, at times, meet and beat the best turkey hunters in a locality season after season. You go into a turkey's domain with shotgun and call, you locate him and challenge him, and do your best to kill him—one on one. You do this *without* bait, highpower scope rifles, fixed or permanent blinds, other hunters, good plots, live turkey decoys, roost shooting, tree houses, etc.

I knew where a high, well-timbered ridge ran through the heart of the best turkey range in the area. I had frequently hunted small game along this ridge and knew turkeys regularly roosted in the locality. I walked down this ridge to within 150 yards of the point where it abruptly ended at the swamp's edge. It was still dark except for the eastern horizon. I groped around until I located a large pine to sit by. I sat down, chalked my turkey call, loaded my 20-gauge, and began to owl. A real owl answered and lit in a tree close by. He began to hoot and soon had other owls answering him. After several minutes of owl talk, a turkey gobbler let out his spine-tingling gobble. Gabe says the war cry of the American Indian is copied from the wild turkey's gobble. I don't know what the war cry of an Indian would do to a man but there is no doubt about the effect of a turkey's gobble. When this turkey gobbled directly down my ridge at the swamp's edge, it seemed the temperature suddenly dropped 20 degrees.

It was getting light now and the place where I sat seemed to be too exposed. I dared not move, so I scratched off a series of fast yelps on my box. The gobbler didn't answer and I began to worry that he didn't hear my call. My eyes were glued on the point of my ridge next to the swamp. I didn't see the gobbler come up on the ridge but suddenly he was there and went into a full strut. Gabe said you can tell the age of a turkey by the way he struts. The young ones have trouble lining up all their feathers to present an even, symmetrical show of form. When he begins to strut for the first time, he looks ragged and out of shape. If practice makes perfect, then a turkey gobbler should wind up with a perfect strut because he spends most of his spring days strutting. Well, my turkey's strut told me I had the boss turkey of these parts on my hands. A terrible feeling of inadequacy came over me—me, a teenager, up against him, the toughest turkey in the township. The turkey would stop strutting for a few minutes and stand tall to look. Then he would gobble and start his strutting again. After what seemed hours he began to move toward me, but instead of coming directly down my ridge, he was veering off to my left. He would end up directly to my left and about 80 yards away, by guess.

For about thirty minutes, this gobbler intimidated me with his strutting, drumming, and gobbling. I was too scared to move; but, when I shut my right eye, the increased range of my left eye would catch glimpses of him. He never came in range; and, as I thought it out, I realized I had committed a serious error. Gabe had carefully stressed the point of having your gun between your knees before the turkey shows up. It's too late to rearrange things after a turkey appears even if he is a hundred yards or more away. Suddenly the strutting stopped and I could

The turkey would stop
strutting for a few minutes and
stand tall to look.

The prettiest sight your eyes will ever see.

hear him walking away from me. Silence took over and thoughts tumbled through my mind. I was almost glad this old turkey was gone. Why did I have to draw him in the first place? Why not a one-year-old or a two-year-old? My thoughts always turned to Gabe and that helped me no end. After all, didn't I have the greatest turkey hunter in my corner? Gabe had said many times "the more you are soundly thrashed by a turkey, the better turkey hunter you'll be. It's the most important part of your training."

I made up my mind to sit right where I was till noon. I stretched my legs out and relaxed for a few minutes. My relaxing was cut short by the gobble of my turkey. He was almost in the same place where I'd heard him earlier in the morning. When I gave him a series of yelps, it started an exact duplicate of the earlier encounter. This time, however, he came down the right side of the ridge to make a stand. Later, I detailed my fray with this gobbler to Gabe. Gabe said the way this gobbler traveled the side of the ridge proved him to be a smart old turkey. He will turkey trot, head and body close to the ground, just enough on the side of the ridge to be out of sight. When he reaches a tree or bush to his liking, he will stop and slowly ease his head up to give him a full view of the top of the ridge as well as a good way down the other side. If it was this turkey's purpose to wear me down, he was doing it in great fashion. I wished I was somewhere else. When he again went back to the swamp I thought it was all over and I breathed a sigh of relief. But, would you believe, no sooner had he reached the edge of the swamp, he boomed another gobble? Again I scratched off a series of yelps the best I could. My gobbler instantly responded with a gobble and at the same time appeared on my ridge. I was well positioned; slumped down in front of the big pine, knees drawn up, feet apart, gun resting between knees pointed in his direction, cap pulled so low I was looking through about a one-half-inch opening between knee and cap bill. Slowly he came down the ridge straight toward me. His wings were dropped almost to the ground in kind of a half strut. He would stop about each ten steps, stand tall, and survey the whole scene. Magnificent—the prettiest sight these eyes had seen up to then or, for that matter, since. I eased the hammer back on my 20-gauge single-barrel. The 20-gauge seemed mighty small for this monstrous turkey. I wished for Jay Delk's double-barrel 10-gauge and believe I would have fired both barrels at once and risked being kicked to kingdom come. I kept the turkey covered by my gun sight and that wasn't hard, as he was approaching in a fairly straight course. At twenty-eight steps he stopped and slowly stretched his neck to full length. I remembered Gabe's outline of a turkey with neck stretched. Gabe drew this on a piece of cardboard to stress an important point. He had me shoot this picture aiming at the turkey's head. We counted the number of shot hitting vital areas. Then he had me shoot again, aiming at a point halfway between the turkey's head and the base of the neck. This last shot at the center of the neck had fully one third more shot in vital areas. Gabe said to make the turkey stand tall to get the maximum results. I thought at the time how tough it would be to make a turkey gobbler do anything, but it can be done.

When I squeezed the trigger of my 20-gauge single, the turkey folded and collapsed like a wet dish rag. I bounded from my position and had little trouble getting the instep of my boot on the turkey's neck, just behind his head. Then he began to flop and beat his wings fiercely and I was glad of the coaching I had received on this point. When you stand on a turkey this way he is helpless and you won't get spurred or beat up by the powerful wings. After he quit thrashing, I took my pocket knife, opened his mouth, and cut his throat from the inside. I then hung him head down to bleed. I was so worn out at that point that I lay down on the ground to try to regain my strength. What a battle and what a victory! Now you'll recall what I said at the outset of this account about a fabulous success at the start of my turkey-hunting career. I couldn't stay still very long. Although I was physically worn to a frazzle, my mind was in a storm. Consider the odds I had bucked: fifteen years of age, first time to try to call a wild turkey, called up this trophy turkey three times the same morning, cleanly killed him with one shot from a 20-gauge gun. Incredible.

After a while I took my turkey from the limb he hung on, to examine him closely. He had a beard of twelve inches or more and long, curved, sharp spurs. Gabe would be mighty proud of me and I wished he could have been there. However, Gabe was not likely to be found at this time of year. He would be off camping by himself in some remote area, looking for some wise old gobbler to challenge. Perhaps he would be at one of his favorite places, the Cedar Hammock Community.

This event took place over fifty years ago and I have made reruns through my mind thousands of times since. Little did I know then the price I would pay for this lucky beginning. Success, like the sword of Damocles, to hang over me for a lifetime. The challenge of trying to repeat or beat this feat. Something had to be pushing me past my normal self. An intangible something that I never could quite understand. I simply had to spend a part of my life studying, hunting, and observing the wild turkey.

It seems that when life ceased in this first turkey gobbler, he transferred to me something of his nature, perhaps his wildness. Otherwise, why would I continue to hunt the wild turkey at such an awesome personal sacrifice. Take the Great Depression of the 1930s. I had left the farm for what I thought was a surer way to make a living. Working eighty to ninety hours per week didn't keep me from hunting the wild turkey. From the initial success I kept going downhill fast. For several years, I ran into turkey after turkey that whipped me every conceivable way. Gabe said I was getting a double dose of humility: one from the Great Depression, the other from the turkeys I challenged.

Hen and gobbler tracks.

2

The Wildlife Community

AS the springs rolled by, Gabe and I became good friends. He possessed a rare knowledge and I wanted to gain any part or all of it. I soon learned how to get Gabe to share with me this information I so desired. When with him, I learned by my silence to invite him to make conversation. I read later where someone said, "you ain't learning when you're talking." How true that was and more especially when a pupil and a master were in company with each other. Now, Gabe wasn't what could be classified as a talkative person. Mostly, he would be put in the silent class. He didn't shower you with knowledge but rather dripped it on you. I heard of an ancient torture whereby a drop of water would hit a person's head at very slow intervals, driving him insane. Well, Gabe's knowledge fell kind of like that, only it was gratefully received.

I had been hunting, fishing, and roaming the great outdoors all my life. I saw and heard perhaps the same things as most others who lived the same way. I observed the flushed quail and the flashing flag of the frightened deer. I could stalk the squirrel and other small creatures. I saw the world of nature with the eyes of an amateur observer but with little or no penetration into its inner secrets. It's amazing how very little I saw when all around me there was an explosion of activity.

I was to learn that Gabe's world was made up of a vast series of communities. His community may cover an area of a hundred or two acres or six or eight square miles. I never quite under-

stood his method of division. Anyway we'll take the Cedar
Hammock Community to illustrate. It was bounded on the west
by cold, clear Cedar Creek, on the north by pasture land, on the
south by a rural road, and on the east by a range of rugged,
steep-timbered hills. It covered an area of approximately twelve-
hundred acres. Gabe said it was the finest game range to be
found. We spent many hours in this wildlife paradise. Now
Gabe didn't say "community" when referring to one of his
areas; he would say we're going to Cedar Hammock tomorrow.
The community was my idea and was taken from one of his
descriptions of an area.

Gabe said, think of the wildlife of an area as a rural community of people. Within its borders people are born, live, and
die without getting very far from their birthplace. It is a complex place. The young and the old, the smart and the dumb,
the gossips, the silent ones, the workers, the loafers, and the
alarmists. All different and yet all have one thing in common,
they know what goes on in their area.

When an outsider enters a community of people, his presence
becomes known quickly from one end of the area to the other.
You enter the wildlife community and the shock waves of your
presence vibrate to every corner. Now that is where a great difference sets about. If you know how to approach, enter, and
conduct yourself while there, it will make all the difference in
the world. Matter of fact, if you don't do it right, you won't see
the real wildlife community and the wonder of it all. You'll see
the stage but not the actors.

Gabe asked me, "How important is it for you to see and hear
what goes on in Cedar Hammock?" He knew what my answer
was. I wanted to more than see and hear, I wanted to be a part
of Cedar Hammock. Well, that ain't easy, says Gabe. You'll
have to learn to walk such a smooth fluid movement that you
don't seem to be moving at all, like the wild turkey. At times
you will have to make a big, out-of-the-way circle to get to
where you want to be because a trio of deer are playing hop-
scotch on your regular route. You'll be patient and quiet and
will take the time to study and learn the creatures and their
habits. You'll be able to select a large tree with rugged trunk

Gobbler tracks

A deer picked up your
scent in the dim dawn and
whistled a warning to the gobbler
you had just started gobbling.

and limbs so you can blend in to sit motionless by it for hours. When all these things come to be natural with you, then you begin to enjoy the wildlife community as few people ever have. We all know how the pressures of modern society keep many of us from discovering nature. It is a time-consuming education. Still many do not know how to use the time they do have to best advantage. Gabe could have taught them.

Gabe's communities were colorful in both name and content. Dry Creek, Running Creek, Frost Bridge, Mill Creek, Sulphur Springs, Millers Ridge, to name a few. One thing all these places had in common was the fact that each contained a drove of wild turkeys. Gabe said, of all the creatures in an area, the turkey was the best at using his neighbors to his own advantage. Start to keep track of the times some of the turkey's allies caused you to lose a kill. The time a fine gobbler was almost in gun range and a gray squirrel told him of your presence. How a deer picked up your scent in the dim dawn and whistled a warning to the gobbler you had just started gobbling. The community gossip, the crow, is a past master at tending other creatures' business and the turkey knows how to use that to his own advantage. Fact is, says Gabe, no creature uses those around him as skillfully as the turkey. A deer may think every man is a tree but a turkey would be more likely to think every tree is a man. The excited chattering of the blue jay, the wren, the robin, or any other of these busybodies puts the turkey on notice and in effect puts a kind of shield of protection around him.

Once a gobbler reaches old age, he has become so cautious he is a real challenge to even the best turkey hunters. The old turkey, being just that, was Gabe's specialty. Gabe knew many turkeys by name and location. Once a turkey reaches old age, he quits roaming about as the two-, three-, and four-year-olds are prone to do. He stays pretty much in a given territory, becomes known to Gabe, and joins Gabe's list of "wanted old men." Every wild turkey is a rugged individualist; once he reaches old age, he becomes a real character and his peculiar ways earn him a name. Over the years I learned about certain character turkeys who were able to hold their own with hunter after hunter, year after year. I know some of it seems to border on getting careless with the truth. I don't try to convince anyone that it is so. Most of it came from Gabe's bag of memories. One thing I'll say for a certain fact, I never caught Gabe in a lie.

As the years rolled by, I, too, have run into some real characters, men and turkeys, that I can vouch for. That's one reason I decided to put my facts in a book.

3

Continuing Education

IF you read this book cover to cover, you may learn a thing or two about the wild turkey. From the jumble of words, you may detect that the writer could have spent more time in school. The schools I attended were mostly rural and sat in somewhat of a wildlife area. How could I know then I would need to know how to construct a sentence. It seemed more important to learn how the pair of blue jays put together their home in a tree right outside the window of my English classroom.

They say about ten percent of the fishermen catch ninety percent of the fish. I believe about the same percent would apply to turkey hunting. This percent, of course, applies only to the hunters who are trying to kill their turkey by Gabe's rules. Hunting from fixed blinds or houses on food plots, hunting over bait or picking off turkeys with hi-powered scoped rifles, would radically change the percent. My hat is off to the many people I have known who hunt by the rules. Some of them go year after year and never get a shot at a wild turkey. Some get shots at turkeys but don't bag any. If you shoot at turkeys but don't kill them, perhaps the advice of Gabe would be in order.

A very prominent man of our area became interested in hunting the wild turkey. He had the choice of some of the best turkey range to hunt. It would seem his chance of success would be certain. He worked hard to learn to call the turkey. He became successful in getting the turkey in range but couldn't make the kill. One day as Gabe and I sat in front of this little crossroads store, Mr. V.I.P. came along. He stopped when he saw Gabe. Gabe already had heard of this man's plight and was not surprised when the man laid it out. V.I.P. recounted the many times he had worked up a turkey within range and couldn't kill him. Gabe listened attentively. I figured Gabe knew all along what the problem was. Gabe was not one to throw his knowledge around loosely. Gabe said simply, "You are trying to outdraw a turkey." Gabe continued, "You can't do it - I can't do it - this boy here (indicating me) can't do it - none of the famous gun fighters of the old west could have done it - Mister, it can't be done." Of course, Gabe was referring to the crucial act of bringing the gun in position to aim and fire at a wild turkey who is in shotgun range.

Gabe carefully laid out his patented way of sitting to a turkey. The selection of a body-size tree, the sitting flat down in front of tree, the slumping down while drawing knees up in front, the spreading apart of the feet, the laying of the gun between the knees; then with cap pulled down, you are in the best position to be approached by a turkey gobbler. You have selected a place where you can see and it is important to see your turkey as soon as you can, preferably seventy-five yards or more. You keep him covered with your gun at all times. You have determined before sitting down how close he needs to be to make the kill. A quick appraisal of objects within a thirty-step circumference of your tree tells you when he is in range.

You can move your gun to follow the turkey as he approaches, provided it is moved so very, very slowly. Some people are so awed by turkeys they say this can't be done. Gabe laughs at this. He says some people believe a turkey to be supernatural and this amuses Gabe no end. He says the turkey doesn't need to be given credit for powers he doesn't have; just recognize him for what he is and for what he can do. That's enough; in fact, almost too much.

I sat back, drinking in every word and studying every expression of these two great men. What a contrast—this bronzed lean ramrod-straight countryman and this successful, slightly overweight, overworked business leader. I thought how evenly matched they were—where one would seem to have the edge in this, the other would have the edge in that.

Gabe continued his coaching of Mr. V.I.P. and included the squeeze-trigger aimed shot at the middle of the turkey's neck. Now Gabe said, if your approaching turkey makes you out and suddenly spooks and heads off for parts remote, please don't shoot him because you won't bag him. Perhaps you would put enough shot in his caboose to cause him to suffer for a couple of days and die or be caught by a predator. When you don't get a good shot at your turkey, tell him as he departs, "that's inning one, we'll play another inning - perhaps tomorrow." Summing up, Gabe said "Don't shoot a turkey strutting, running, or flying."

Now Gabe comes up with one of his stories to make his point. "You know," he started, "Tobe Sill the colored man who is known far and wide for his uncanny ability to bag quail on the wing. It is said that Tobe averages twenty-five quail for every box of twenty-five shells he shoots. His ability to pick out two or three quail in a shot pattern on a covey ups his average. Now you know that takes extraordinary reflexes and eyesight. Well, Tobe said to me one day that he would like for me to call-up him a turkey. He had heard the stories of the turkey's ability to outdo a man in the game of quick draw. Tobe wanted to match skills with Mr. Gobbler."

Gabe said he took Tobe to one of his favorite spots and early that morning a gobbler was challenging the world with his gobbling. Gabe told Tobe where to sit and then Gabe moved back about fifty yards to do the calling. Tobe said he wanted to give the turkey a fair chance so he would simply lay his gun in his lap until the turkey got in range. Tobe had said many times, "won't no turkey alive can come up within thirty steps that I can't get a killing shot at."

Gabe soon realized that two gobblers were answering his calls and were on their way toward Tobe and him. The ridge where Gabe and Tobe sat was fairly open, with huge long-bodied pines scattered along its crown. Patches of waist-high bushes and broom sedge covered the ground. Gabe saw the gobblers off to one side of the ridge and they were circling toward Tobe. Their tacking and circling finally brought them up behind Tobe and in front of Gabe. They were about ten yards directly behind Tobe's tree and there they started their show.

The two gobblers were in their prime—fine, well-proportioned three-year-olds. Back and forth they marched behind Tobe's tree, gobbling, strutting, and drumming. Now this can be a most nervewracking ordeal for the most experienced turkey hunter. To a less experienced person, it could easily be a hazard to his health. The indians who patterned their war cry after the gobbling of the wild turkey well knew what it took to curdle a person's blood.

Gabe was enjoying this show no end. He had no gun and was in position to see every move. Gabe knew this couldn't go on for long - something had to give. After about ten minutes, it happened. Now Tobe Sill was no novice to the ways of the wild. Tobe was a good woodsman in his own right. Frankly though, he wasn't prepared for what was taking place. When Tobe heard the gobbler answer Gabe, he braced himself for the confrontation he knew would come. Tobe's keen eyes had seen the turkey slipping along the side of the ridge and he froze in position as Gabe had told him he must do. Of course, the circle the turkeys made soon took them out of sight. The next thing he knew, the turkey (Tobe didn't know there were two turkeys) was behind him and, as he said later, carrying on something awful.

Tobe said, every now and then, he would catch a glimpse of the turkey as he came part way down the ridge only to turn and retrace his route. Tobe said his whole body was a-shaking and he simply was being sapped of his strength. He finally decided while he had the strength to make his move, he must act. The next time he caught a glimpse of the turkey he would roll out from behind the tree, raise to one knee, and bag his tormentor. Tobe figured the turkey would be about fifteen steps to his left, with the element of surprise in Tobe's favor. A few moments later out of the corner of his eye, Tobe saw the turkey and made his move. As Gabe said later, Tobe did a good job of rolling out

Back and forth they marched behind Tobe's tree, gobbling, strutting and drumming.

If your turkey makes you out and takes off running or flying ~ let him go ~ try him another day.

and raising to one knee with gun in position. There was only one thing wrong; when Tobe got in position, there simply was no turkey to be seen. Tobe seemed frozen in this stance, up on one knee, gun to shoulder and aiming at space. Gabe said he wished for a kodak as this would have been a dilly of a picture.

As Gabe started toward Tobe, he realized what a price poor Tobe had paid for his part in this game of quick draw. Tobe's eyes seemed twice their normal size and he was shaking all over. When Tobe gained some of his composure, he asked Gabe simply, "Did you see a turkey?" Gabe didn't want to make matters worse than they were so he said nothing about there being two turkeys. "Yes, Tobe, there was a fine gobbler right behind you when you tumbled out from behind the tree."

Tobe reenacted the whole scene several times. Each time he would come up shaking his head and saying weakly, "I don't believe it." Gabe even tried to help Tobe's feelings by explaining that the back side approach the turkey made was not in Tobe's best interest. You could tell that Tobe's feelings for the whole affair bordered on the supernatural. The turkeys had made a believer out of Tobe because he told Gabe, "Mr. Gabe, what you say about the turkey is so. He flat know how to take care of hisself. What chance you got with something that can vaporate right before your eyes?"

Mr. V.I.P. listened to Gabe intently. This important man didn't get where he was by ignoring or taking expert advice lightly. He, of course, knew that Gabe was telling it like it was. Mr. V.I.P. did in fact become an expert turkey hunter in his own right and was not the least bit ashamed to give Gabe Meadow due credit for his success.

After Mr. V.I.P. had gotten to be a good turkey hunter, I heard him make a statement that made a big impression on me. It has stayed with me all my life. This big man said: "Of all the big game animals in all the world, the bagging of an old turkey gobbler is the most difficult." Mr. V.I.P. then made it clear that he was talking about turkey hunting by Gabe's rules. He went on to say that he had hunted and killed at least one of most all big game animals on every continent. No matter how far he got from the wild turkey, he always came back to hunt him, realizing that he is in fact the king. "Man, when you go after an old gobbler, proper like, you are playing in the big league," he said. He would go on to give you some good reasons for the degree of difficulty.

When you hunt a wild turkey consider these factors:

1. The game is going to be played on the turkey's home field.
2. He can see ten times better than you.
3. He can hear five times better than you.
4. He can outrun you even when wounded.
5. He can rocket into space on powerful wings at a moment's notice.
6. Every bird in his territory is his ally.
7. Every animal in his territory is his ally.
8. Every insect in his territory is his ally.
9. He is a better physical specimen than you.
10. His endurance is better than yours.
11. His patience is superior.
12. His motive for winning the game is better than yours; to you a game, to him life itself.
13. His thought process is radically different from yours. The more you try to figure him out, the more you believe the saying "crazy as a loon" should be changed to "crazy as a wild turkey."
14. Every second you are in contact with a mature gobbler, events and circumstances take place, any one of which could have a direct bearing on your losing the game.

These are just a few reasons why an old wild-turkey gobbler offers such a challenge. When you hunt him, you will add many more reasons of your own to this list.

After I had hunted the wild turkey for about twenty years, I figured everything that could happen to keep me from making a kill had happened. My fifty-third season to hunt the wild turkey just passed and I added more reasons for failure, perhaps more this season than during any other season. Although I have killed over two hundred wild-turkey gobblers during my life, I make no claim as to my rating with other turkey hunters. I do, however, here and now post my claim to having more alibis than any other turkey hunter, living or dead. There is no way for another turkey hunter to beat me in this area. I have alibis stacked so neatly and closely in the back of my head that I believe this has inspired IBM to come up with the memory bank for their computer.

4

The Saga of Gallberry Joe

SOME five or six years had passed since I killed my first turkey. At the opening of each spring turkey season thereafter, I was ready to continue my turkey learning. I hunted mostly alone but always had Gabe to fall back on for advice and encouragement. Although he never said so, I knew Gabe took great satisfaction in my developing as a turkey hunter.

An event happened along about this time that sent my stock soaring with Gabe. Down south of us lay Lane County and there was some real turkey hunting in that county. Lane County also had some good turkey hunters, many of whom were friends of Gabe's. One day one of these hunters passed our way and got in touch with Gabe to do some turkey talking. This man by the name of Able Downey wasn't long in telling Gabe about a certain turkey in their part of the country who was outwitting all who challenged him. For the past three years every turkey hunter in that part of the country had learned about him and many had tried to kill him.

Now back in those times when there were just a few turkey hunters and not too many turkeys, a turkey could gain a reputation. If a certain turkey was hunted and survived one season, he was on his way to fame. For each season he managed to survive the hunter's challenge, his fame grew. If a great amount of pressure was put on him by good turkey hunters and he still walked his domain proud and free after three years, then he became a local celebrity—a celebrity at least in the eyes of turkey hunters. To other people like young brides, old wives, preachers, bosses, creditors, and sweethearts, he could be a downright villain. When these turkeys gained their fame and celebrity status, they usually also were given a name which became their trademark.

The turkey Mr. Downey was talking about had earned both a name and a reputation. His name was Gallberry Joe. Mr. Downey went on to explain that Gallberry Joe earned his name from the fact that he spent all his time in an area almost completely covered by chest-high gallberry bushes. In this part of the country, the evergreen gallberry grows in profusion and grows well even in the shade of the longleaf pine. Gabe's interest in Gallberry Joe grew as Mr. Downey told of the many good turkey hunters from over Mississippi and Alabama and other places who had challenged Gallberry Joe. It was kind of an unwritten agreement among turkey hunters to let other hunters try for an old turkey who had gained such fame. Gabe told Mr. Downey, "Me and this boy might come down and have a look see at Mr. Gallberry Joe."

After Mr. Downey left, Gabe turned to me and said simply, "We'll try Gallberry Joe, Boy." Gabe had already explained the procedure for going into a strange territory to hunt. He explained that the local hunters had the first chance each year to hunt a named turkey. After they had kind of given up, then they would usually let you try for him. Now this sounds like all turkey hunters make up a great family of congenial people. I don't intend to give that impression at all, because it just ain't so. There has always existed among turkey hunters a certain jealousy, a certain amount of backbiting, a lot of false information designed to throw one off track, and an unbelievable amount of downright lying. A case in point.

In this very area where Gallberry Joe made his reputation, there lived a turkey hunter by the name of Tony McCleb. Gabe said in his prime, Tony was a real master turkey hunter. Now he was able to hunt very little, being ninety years old and the victim of arthritis. Tony's mind was still good and he could spin a turkey yarn with the best. He told Gabe, in confidence, how for many years he lived about ten miles from Daleboro, the

county seat of Lane County. Daleboro had a bunch of avid turkey hunters who covered the surrounding area like the dew.
Tony had carved him a hugh turkey foot and fixed it so he could
attach it to his walking stick. During the weekdays, Tony
walked the sand roads and trails of the whole area, implanting
this "big foot" as he called it. He systematically walked big
foot in the areas where no turkeys were to be found. Come
weekends, the town fellows would be scouting and making
mental notes of turkey signs. Tony said the more he walked big
foot, the worst would be his justice due were he caught. Most
turkey hunters will erase or cover over turkey tracks they find
when scouting. I can imagine the great confusion of some of
these hunters who on opening day would be in the area where
they had repeatedly found tracks of this huge gobbler, Big Foot.

When Gabe and I arrived in Daleboro the season had been
open a couple of weeks. Sure enough, Gallberry Joe had again
been busy whipping the daylights out of the local hunters. Gabe
had the respect of these hunters, because they agreed to let us
try for Gallberry Joe. One of them volunteered to take us out to
Joe's stomping grounds. We were traveling in Gabe's old pickup truck and, at last, I would get to camp out with Gabe. That
in itself was to be an education. He had told me, "Just bring
yourself a change of clothes." We drove out to this remote area
and parked the truck. From there we walked about a half mile
to the domain of Gallberry Joe.

It was beautiful country, well timbered on the ridges and valleys. The beautiful longleaf pine timbered the ridges, and the
valleys were mostly mixed hardwood. Under the trees, the
whole area was nearly covered by the evergreen gallberry bush.
We scouted the area carefully. The man who showed the place
to us said we could hear Gallberry Joe from an old logging
road which ran the length of the highest ridge in the area.
Gabe followed the man along this road and surveyed the battle-
ground. No detail, even the smallest, would escape the keen
eyes of Gabe Meadow. His eyes absorbed it all and fed it to his
brain for storage and future use.

I, too, was looking for all I was worth and I wasn't liking what
I saw. The gallberry bushes literally covered the whole area.

They grew in patches with lanes between. Try as I would, I could never find a place where you could see more than thirty or forty feet in any direction. Most of the bushes were waist high or higher. The logging road itself wound down the ridge and you couldn't see very far down it. I thought, here we were challenging this turkey before every turkey hunter in Lane County. You could bet all these local turkey hunters would be pulling for Gallberry Joe. The more I thought about it, the weaker I became on our chances. I believed Gabe was the best turkey hunter alive, but even he couldn't perform miracles. How could anybody kill a smart turkey that you couldn't see? Worse, here we were down in Lane County, which sort of said to the locals, "Boys, we are down here to show y'all how to kill a smart turkey." We walked the logging road to where it played out at the edge of a swamp, then turned and retraced our route to the truck.

Gabe thanked the man who pointed out the area to us and we set about making camp. Gabe said thoughtfully "After supper, we'll ride over and have a talk with Tony McCleb. I want you to get to know him. He may know some of the tactics that have been used on Gallberry Joe. Maybe also he'll spin a yarn or two for your benefit." Nothing could have pleased me more. I never have had enough of turkey talk even to this day. Back then it was even better; and when the talkers were master turkey hunters, well, you couldn't beat that.

It didn't take us long to eat the light supper Gabe prepared. One egg each, two pieces of bacon cut from a slab, and a hoecake. The hoecake was a kind of biscuit cooked in a skillet, and real good. Gabe said we didn't come to eat but to hunt. I didn't comment, as the fact seemed evident.

When we pulled up in front of Tony McCleb's house, it was dusk dark. It was not too dark to take note of Tony's house. The house was typical of these parts except older. It was built with a dog trot or open hall running all the way through the house. The lumber was heart pine, wide boards that had never been painted. A porch, the width of the house, was at the front and back. I think most of the bedrooms were on one side. Along the walls of the hall hung all kinds of farm needs: tools, baskets, buckets, hats, other items of clothing and an assortment of gadgets.

Tony McCleb met us at the door of the sitting room and ushered us inside. In the huge fireplace blazed the brightest fire I ever saw. There was no other light in the room nor was it needed. I soon discovered it was a pine knot fire. The corner of the room contained three huge cotton baskets piled high with the knots. Most of these knots are cone shaped. Instead of using dogirons, the knots were piled in the center of the fireplace with the small end up. The heat and light they gave off was amazing. I knew some of the big lumber companies fired their steam locomotives with pine knots and now I saw why. They put out tremendous heat.

When Gabe introduced me to Tony, he said, "This here boy is a turkey hunter." That was the first time I was given this title and it made me real proud. I thought, what an honor it is to be in the company of these two master turkey hunters. Of course, I would say nothing but rather would drink in every word that passed between these two great men. Tony McCleb was small framed; you could tell he had been around for a few winters. Still, he got about pretty good for those ninety years.

As I studied Mr. Tony, I noted his remarkable eyes. He wore no glasses and his bright eyes flashed a fire belying his many years. Back in those days in the rural sections of the country, there was very little entertainment of the kind we have today. No TV, no movies, no autos to ride in, no newspapers, very few books and magazines, poor to no radios. People simply entertained each other. I guess every community had its natural entertainers in the form of people who had a talent for it. Some had fantastic memories and could entertain any audience with their colorful accounts of the past. Tony McCleb was gifted in this respect. With his great age and good memory he could take you way back to the true pioneer days. Three subjects have always fascinated me: turkeys, Indians, and the old days. Small wonder when Tony McCleb combined the three in his colorful style, my joy knew no bounds. Who else in the world would be as qualified as he to tell about them.

Along about the time Tony was born, the U.S. Government made treaties with the native Indians of this area to acquire the land from them. Most of the Indians were moved from the area. Tony said quite a few McClebs and people related to them came from South Carolina to homestead and settle the land. The settlers were a hardy lot with one common trait: the desire to help and be helped by their fellow man. Hence they permitted the Indians who had been moved from the area to return for visits to their old hunting grounds. Tony, as a boy, played, fished, and hunted with these Indians. Quite a few Indian families would come each year to camp on the colorful Sucarnoochee River. They made all kinds of baskets and the large wooden bowls so desired and useful to the pioneer housewife. Tony thus had access to a phase of turkey hunting not available to most.

It is a proven fact that the Indian hunted the wild turkey for hundreds of years before the white man ever heard of an Indian or a turkey. Not only did the Indian hunt the wild turkey but he did it with an enthusiam probably challenging that of the most avid turkey hunter of today. The Indian clearly had all the motives for the hunt we have, plus the added motive of self-survival. Consider what an English writer who died in the late 1700s had to say about the Indian and the wild turkey. "Savage man seems to find a delight in precarious possession. A great part of the pleasure of the chase lies in the uncertainty of the pursuit." This English writer of over 200 years ago, thus points out in his unique style the most important and fascinating part of hunting the wild turkey: "The uncertainty of the pursuit." Now after over fifty years of hunting the wild turkey, I hereby swear that the pursuit remains uncertain.

Tony, like most turkey hunters of his day, didn't go around sharing the secrets of his success with everyone. Through trial and error, he developed his techniques and hid them in the back of his mind. Tony said a few years ago, a group of men from Daleboro came out to get him to settle a great argument. It seems a man came through Daleboro selling turkey calls. The salesman claimed that one of his calls was an exact copy of the turkey calls used by the Indian. This group of men wanted Tony to tell them if, in fact, the turkey call that one man in the group had purchased was the original Indian turkey call.

Now foxy old Tony would not make any positive statement of fact when talking about the wild turkey or its hunting. Like a good lawyer, he would qualify his statements with such ambiguity as to protect himself from having made any positive statements. Tony listened to both sides of the argument and made his observation. "Boys," he said, "I've hunted wild turkeys with the Indians and I never saw one with a turkey call. Now, I'm not saying they didn't have them or use them. One thing I do know for a fact is that an Indian boy of eight or more years could imitate with his natural voice any sound of nature. I mean all the sounds—the rippling water of a creek, the wind in the trees, any bird, any animal. It was an art with them, cherished and appreciated. Why, Boys, I've seen an Indian lay by a log with the fan (tail feathers) of a turkey gobbler open as if in full strut and waving it in the air above the log, and the Indian would be drumming, gobbling, clucking and going on something awful with his mouth. Up could come a wild gobbler and he'd seem to be trying to imitate the Indian. Then up would come another gobbler until several would be around gawking, strutting, gobbling, and going on like you won't believe. After a few minutes of mass confusion, the Indian would jump up and kill one of these gobblers with a stick he had laying by his log. Now, if you still think an Indian used an artificial call, it's all right with me."

As Tony spun his story, I would look at Gabe to see on his face the satisfaction of time being well spent. Tony was just getting warmed up. Gabe knew some stories would have to be listened to before Tony would come up with information on Gallberry Joe. Gallberry Joe. Man, I had almost let him slip my mind as I enjoyed this real turkey talk. But there he was and I knew tough going lay ahead.

Tony said years ago his cousins Zeke and Deak McCleb lived down the road a piece. They both were turkey hunters and pretty good at it. These two boys were so wild and woolly no woman had got up enough nerve to try to tame one of them. They were confirmed bachelors and that suited them because it fitted in well with their lifestyle. They worked a few patches around their cabin and did just enough other work to earn the small amount of money to buy their few needs. The rest of their time they hunted and fished. Like turkey hunters of that day and time, they hunted the wild turkey primarily during spring gobbling time. There was no season or limits. If turkeys took to gobbling during a nice warm sunny spell of weather in January, off the wall would come gun and call. Tony said he didn't want to give the impression Zeke and Deak were tight with their money, but he had heard this long-legged pair was known to step over the yard fence to keep from wearing out the gate hinges. Tony also said he was looking over one of these boys' double-barrel hammer guns. When he looked inside the barrels, he noted one barrel had an obstruction in it. It turned out that a dirt dauber wasp had built a nest in the right barrel. He took it up with Zeke, and Zeke said: "Well, I don't load or shoot but one barrel. Once I had both barrels loaded and somehow shot both at one time, wasting a shell."

Tony continued, "One year during a pretty spell of weather in early spring the wild gobblers took to gobbling, and Zeke and Deak headed to their favorite places. They hunted separate but still near enough to each other to hear each other shoot. It had barcly got light enough to see when Deak heard the boom of Zeke's "Old Betsy" travel the sound waves of the moist crisp spring air. Now its a natural thing for turkey hunting partners to be competitive. When you hear your partner shoot what you believe to be a turkey (probably a trophy one) it kind of sets you on fire to get one yourself. Your mind gets to wandering; your partner gets one this morning and you none. Maybe tomorrow the same thing happens. First thing you know he's got several and you, none. People come by and ask "How you boys doing with turkeys this year?" What are you going to say? It gets to where things run through your mind that ought not to. Tony says, if you don't put this thing to rest, it will get to you and take from you your love for turkey hunting. As soon as you feel a tinge of greed or jealousy start coming up in you, stamp it out like a wild fire. Strong men have broken under this situation.

Shortly after Zeke's first shot, there came another. Deak didn't understand. That's not like Zeke, who would not pull a

trigger until he was sure of a kill. When still another shot rang
out, Deak knew something was wrong and began to make his
way to Zeke. Before he got there, Zeke had fired again. Deak
slipped up behind Zeke to try to see what was going on. Zeke
was behind a huge log, gun resting on it and aimed up a big
hickory tree. Zeke motioned Deak to be quiet, but Deak had to
find out. "What the hell you doing?" he asked Zeke. Under
his breath Zeke replied, "Don't you see that big old crazy gobbler sitting on that hickory limb." Deak now knew it. Zeke was
going crazy. Deak caught Zeke by one of his legs and pulled
him around so he could look at him. Then he saw it. A great
big swamp mosquito was sitting on the rim of Zeke's glasses.
Deak said he always figured Zeke could see better without the
glasses but Zeke insisted on wearing them as he thought they
gave him a kind of scholarly look. Zeke had bought them from
a fellow who travelled through the country selling glasses.

Man, what entertainment. Every thing we had heard about
Tony McCleb was true. I thought: what a vast store of knowledge he had amassed during his ninety years. I then realized
that men like Tony were more than entertainers. In pioneer
days with little formal education available, the Tony McClebs
were the educators as well as the entertainers. If you listened
long enough to these people with their vast experience, you
could learn almost anything: how to court a woman, how to
treat your fellowman, etc., etc. Now all this useful information
didn't come in condensed form. Matter of fact it was mixed in
with a vast amount of other information, some of which you
would be better off not to try to use. Many of the tales were
handed down through the generations and each generation
would add to or delete from them, according to their own
whims. Now that was another part of your education. You
would learn to listen to all this talk and filter fact from fiction
and this may just be the most important thing you could possibly learn.

After Tony finished the Zeke and Deke tale, he sank back into
his huge rocking chair and closed his eyes. Gabe and I sat
silently wondering what would come next from the great res-
ervoir of Tony McCleb's mind. We didn't have to wonder long,

because the words we had hoped to hear started flowing. "I hear you boys are down in these parts to make yourselves known to Gallberry Joe. This here Joe turkey has sure made a name for himself. Why, turkey hunters from far and near have had the same thing on their minds. I guess I have been kind of the score keeper because I get reports from most all who try for old Joe. Then, too, most of these same folks come by before they start hunting Gallberry Joe to see what I know about him. Now Gabe, I know you don't need no advice on turkey hunting so I guess what I say is intended for the boy. What I say has been said before to all who wanted me to have a say about Joe. Now I don't want to underrate Mr. Gallberry Joe and take the pride away from the man who gits him. What makes this turkey double tough is the territory he stays in. You have had a look and Gabe I know you have realized this fact. Joe's territory covers about five hundred acres and looks for the world like a big checker board. The dark squares are the patches of gall-berry bushes. The light squares are the open areas between. This is free range territory and cows roam free. These cows keep the open areas opened up by grazing them year round. This has been going on long as I can remember. Every now and then a gobbler figures out that this place is his best defense against his worst enemy: man. I personally have hunted this area off and on for eighty years and tell you now there has been gobblers who made it to die a natural death in this gallberry jungle. I don't want to discourage you so I'll say also that I took some smart ones out of there and so have some other hunters. This Gallberry Joe has likely seen near every trick known to turkey hunters. So far he has won the game but somebody, maybe this here boy, may come up with something to befuddle old Joe and take him hands down. Now, if I was this boy, I'd try to figure something new to put to Mr. Joe."

Tony looked intently at Gabe to prepare him for his next state-ments. He seemed intent on having Gabe accept what he was about to tell. Tony chose his words carefully, "I've been turkey hunting and turkey watching and turkey this and turkey that for nigh on to eighty years. I have finally come to believe that once a turkey finds out he can whip a man he begins to like to do it.

Now take this Gallberry Joe. When you go into his territory, you ain't going to have no trouble getting up with him. He is going to let you know he is there and ready for you. You are going to hear some of the dangist gobbling and clucking and drumming you ever heard. Why? Because Gallberry Joe wants to challenge you. Now if he didn't want to challenge you all he would have to do would be to set up in the middle of his Gallberry Paradise and you'd never have a chance at him or even know he was there. Don't you believe other creatures beside man like to win?''

I thought, what a lawyer Tony would have made. I doubt though that he would have swapped his full years close to nature for any other way of life. He didn't have to tell you that the path he chose was the right one. Tony then threw in the clincher, proof of his theory. ''Down the road a piece lived a man named Conway Sones. Conway was a deer hunter and always had a big pack of deer hounds. When one of Conway's boys was small, he found this male fawn deer with a broke leg. He took him home and fixed his leg and the boy wanted to keep him. The deer grew to be grown and they made this big pole pen to keep him in and away from the dogs. The deer grew to be a big one and rambunctious. He feuded constantly with the dogs, whistling, snorting, and stamping his feet and running around his pen. One day he had the whole pack of dogs barking and running around the pen. All of a sudden the deer sailed over the fence and headed for the wide open spaces. He led the dogs on a wild chase of four or five miles and when he had enough, he came back and sailed over the fence back into his pen. After that, when the mood struck him, he would start teasing the dogs to get them all riled up so he could sail out of the pen and outrun the pack. There is no doubt that he enjoyed the chase as much as the dogs, maybe more. Next time you see a deer leading a bunch of dogs on a chase, don't feel sorry for him; he likely is enjoying it.''

Gabe admitted that Tony's theory about turkeys enjoying laying it on a man had merit. Gabe said several times he had almost come to the same conclusion. Tony quickly returned to Gallberry Joe and what he knew of him. ''Likely,'' Tony said, "when someone gets Gallberry Joe, he is going to be a mossy-head turkey and not much bigger than that domineck rooster over there by the porch. As I said, you won't have no trouble making contact with him. When you hear him gobble in the morning and set to him, this is what will most apt to happen. He will come toward you, gobbling every few steps to the helping you have given him. It will look like he's going to run over you. When he gets about one hundred steps from you, he will stop gobbling and you won't hear a sound. After he has made you sweat this out for about thirty minutes, he'll run off about two hundred yards to your left and start gobbling. He wants you to come on over and play checkers with him. Every dern one of these turkeys that has stayed in them gallberry bushes does that way. They must all be kin and act alike. Back in the days when I really hunted turkeys and one of these smart devils was holed up in that gallberry jungle, I would waste a lot of time there. Some days I would get so mad I'd stay all day and every time he would move I would move. I figured with both of us moving about, there was bound to be a eyeball-to-eyeball meeting. Somehow it never worked out that way and I could not figure why it didn't."

Gabe had heard enough and arose to make our departure. Each of us gave Mr. Tony a real country handshake, which consists of just one pump of the hand. I never have known why city folks, when shaking hands, will pump and pump each other and country folks give just one good pump. I marvelled at the firm grip of Mr. Tony. What a man he must have been in his younger days.

We were heading for camp and Gabe was in deep thought. We were almost to campsite before Gabe shared his thoughts with me. "We'll get a good night's rest and be ready for this Mr. Gallberry Joe come morning," Gabe reflected. "No matter where you are and intend to hunt," continued Gabe, "you got to have proper rest to do your best. Now, you take these hunting camps with all the comforts of home. They tempt a man to be settin' up in there instead of being out where the game is. These hunting camps have saved the lives of lots of turkeys. Here comes a bunch of hunters to camp and hunt turkeys. The more there are of them, the less turkeys they kill. They bring enough equipment to invade China. They have more whiskey than groceries. They stay up near all night playing poker, smoking, and drinking whiskey. If one gets up at all in the morning, it will be a miracle. But if he does, what chance will this poor, bleary-eyed strength-sapped duffer have when he challenges a wild turkey gobbler? I have thought many times that a good big wild turkey gobbler could flat whip the daylights out of the average man who hunts him. If this turkey would slip up on a hunter and fly into him, beating with his wings and raking with his spurs, it wouldn't take long to decide the winner. One thing for sure, there would be a lot more turkeys and a lot less turkey hunters.''

I knew Gabe had thought about which one of us would hunt Gallberry Joe first. I also knew it would be one of us and not both, because Gabe believed firmly in the one-man-to-one-turkey rule. The long awaited announcement came as Gabe said simply, "You'll hunt Joe tomorrow and if he survives, I'll take him the next day. We'll hunt him that way—you, one day; me, the next—until we settle this thing to everyone's satisfaction.'' The moment of truth had come and butterflies swarmed in my stomach. I had hoped that Gabe would hunt Joe the first day, kill him, and I would be on the team that did it.

I learned many things from this great man, Gabe Meadow. If I had to single out the most important one, it would have to be the way one prepares himself for whatever he expects to come which will test his preparedness. Gabe would say there are just a handful of people in this world who are willing to make the sacrifice of completely preparing themselves for whatever goal they seek. The preparation of mind and body demand an awesome price which most people won't pay. I tried to take heart for the pending battle with the successes I had come by in outwitting some good gobblers. But this Gallberry Joe wasn't a good gobbler or a trophy gobbler. He was a legend in his own lifetime.

I had a fitful night's sleep. Audubon's account of the droves of 1500 wild turkeys grazing on the bluegrass plains of Kentucky invaded my mind. In my dreams, I witnessed a drove of

1500 wild turkeys marching all the way to California by way of Texas. I was trying to count them to prove the accuracy of Audubon's statement, which I always doubted. The counting was almost impossible because every now and then the turkeys would all bunch up and start circling. Faster and faster they would circle until they would be running full steam. Then the circle would spread out, leaving one lone turkey in the center of the circle. This lone turkey, which was about the size of a banty rooster, had a large orange disc painted on one of his wings the way the modern turkey biologist identifies turkeys today. I could see that something was written on this orange disc and it seemed imperative that I find out what the message said—this without disturbing the flock. Finally, on a cue from our Indian friends, I took the fan (tail feathers) of a turkey, attached it to my caboose, and joined the circling turkeys, keeping pace and time with them. They accepted me and I gradually worked my way to the inner part of the circle and close enough to the lone turkey in center to read the message. It read "Gallberry Joe." Damn.

It seemed that I had just drifted off into a deep sleep when Gabe shook me to reality. The standard egg, bacon, hoecake, and coffee was ready and we ate in silence. Gabe always said "You prepare yourself beforehand not at hand." So, true to that theory, Gabe offered no last minute advice. I believe, by his calmness, he was trying to bolster my confidence. It needed bolstering.

When we parted that morning, not one word was spoken. Gabe gave me the pioneer woodsman's parting salute, hand in front of chest, palm down and slowly turning palm up. What this gesture means I don't know, but it was better than words, in turkey territory or, for that matter, better in the pioneer days when woodsmen lived in hostile territories. Sign language was better than the spoken word, obviously.

Silently, I worked my way down the old logging road into Gallberry Joe's territory. The silence of this remote territory waited to be broken by the day shift of creatures who would be taking over shortly. It was a crisp morning and a heavy dew had fallen, deadening sounds of footsteps. After I had moved several hundred yards in Joe's domain, I stopped to wait for more light. The curtain of darkness rose slowly and objects began to take form. I began to owl in a series of hoots. A whip-poor-will began his piercing "chip-fell-off-the-white-oak, chip-fell-off-the-white-oak." A distant owl picked up my imitation and hooted back at me. Slowly Joe's paradise came to life as its citizens talked to each other. The hum of activity made me wonder if I would be able to hear Gallberry Joe's gobble. I knew he would gobble. Mr. McCleb said he would. I thought, if he knew who he had drawn for the day's battle, he would already be gobbling.

Abruptly the area seemed to become silent because above it all a raspy, shrill screech of a gobble sent sound waves into every nook and corner. It was Gallberry Joe and I knew it as well as if he himself had distinctly announced his name. He was about two hundred yards down the ridge and about a hundred yards down the draw that ran parallel with the ridge. I quickly moved down the ridge to a point I felt would be about a hundred yards from his roost tree in the bottom of the valley or draw. At this point, I owled and Joe answered, and he was, in fact, directly down the ridge at the bottom of the draw. I could tell that the gallberry bushes covered this draw in a solid mass at the roost point; but, up toward the crown of the ridge and my road, they thinned out to patches with space between. I had already decided to start my encounter with Joe with one of the oldest yet most effective tactics known to turkey hunters. I gave Joe a soft, rapid series of yelps known by master turkey hunters as the true mating call of the wild turkey hen. Joe answered immediately. As soon as I finished my yelp, I moved silently and very quickly about fifty yards directly toward Joe. Now you can't always use this maneuver due to factors of light and cover; but, when it is possible, it's hard to beat. I heard the whirr of Joe's wings when he glided out of the tree. Also, the thud of his feet when he landed. He landed down the side of the ridge not more than eighty yards from me. My moving up after the yelp had gained about twenty to thirty yards in my favor. With this advantage, I decided to remain silent, hoping he would believe I was still up on the road where I first yelped. I don't know what he really was thinking, but he was giving me the silent treatment.

For thirty minutes this silent cold war continued and I began to realize that Joe was winning it. I owled hoping he would reveal his location as other gobblers had done before him. Silence. Truly, I didn't know what to do but knew I would be no worse off whatever I did. I got down with my box call almost to the ground and gave the yelp and cackle on it. I then eased up about fifteen yards in the direction Joe was, the last time I had heard him hit the ground. About ten minutes later, the silence was shattered by Joe's shrill gobble. Would you believe he was up in the logging road at the top of the ridge and almost at the point where I had first yelped to him. How he got there I don't know.

Joe now began to run a pattern familiar to many who hunt turkeys. He gobbled at a certain point in the road on top of the ridge. In about five minutes he had moved about 75 yards down the ridge to another point where he gobbled again. Then he returned to the first point and gobbled. He was running a specific route in about the same place and upon reaching each end of his route, he would gobble. Or would it be that he would gobble just before leaving the end of his route? How long would he take to make the seventy-five yard run? Would he stop frequently between the ends of his route to look? You were certain of only one thing and that is there was a turkey out there running a pattern and gobbling at each end. Everything else you have to guess at. Old turkeys will do this running-from-point-to-point routine for several minutes and sometimes for hours. Back and forth, back and forth. Gabe called this "running a pattern" and at times it can work in your favor. Gabe taught me to study the pattern of the turkey's route and timing. You have it fixed in your mind so when the turkey arrives at one point, you move quickly and quietly a short way toward the opposite point. Carefully you are working your way toward getting in range of your turkey.

A word of caution here. Moving around this close to a turkey gobbler is extremely hazardous and should be attempted only when everything else fails. A turkey acting this way is doubly

alert, suspicious, and has his senses revved up to maximum ef-
ficiency. Every time Joe gobbled at the end of his route farthest
from me, I crawled a short distance toward the opposite end.
This crawling around in rattlesnake country is kind of nervewracking and I halfway expected to come up eye ball to eye ball
with the biggest one in these parts. People who picked cotton
wore knee pads. Gabe said some turkey hunters needed them
worse than the cotton pickers. Some crawlers became so pro-
ficient at crawling, they could drop down from hand and knees
to flat on the stomach and slither and squirm along like a snake
or worm.

Although the crawlers at times amused Gabe, he had little
respect for the ones who used this technique almost exclusively.
One man in our area crawled so much during his hunting that
he earned the name of Crawling Sam Ames. Once during a jam
session of turkey hunters, Crawling Sam expressed concern
about running into a rattlesnake. Gabe told him "Why Sam, I
don't believe you would be in any danger. You crawl around so
much, I believe the other crawlers would accept you as one of
them. Maybe a big boar rattlesnake may try to lay a little love
on you—you should watch out for that."

I was almost at the point where I thought Joe would be in
range if I could see him. I dared not move another inch until
Joe gobbled again. The expected gobble didn't come. I waited
and the minutes rolled by, each one taking its toll of my
strength and confidence. After about twenty minutes, Joe let
out his war cry at a point about two hundred yards down the
logging road and he had passed the point where I was in reaching his new position. I should have known that this turkey was
going to give me a lesson I would never forget. I was trying to
match wits with him, using sheer guesswork against brilliant,
deliberately planned strategy. Now what if General Robert E.
Lee had had this durn turkey give him some pointers. You see,
even now almost a half century later, it is difficult to stay with
the subject of Gallberry Joe because his very memory blows my
mind.

One time that morning, Joe succeeded in pinning me down in
an area almost completely covered with gallberry bushes. I

could barely see ten steps in any direction. At that point, he approached me gobbling every few steps until it seemed he was literally on top of me. There he began his strutting and drumming. I could hear his wings scraping the ground as he strutted. Finally when he again departed my company and gobbled about three hundred yards down the side of the ridge, I decided to break off our engagement. Mixed emotions clouded my mind, among them humility and anger. I reached the logging road and had gone a short distance when I noticed a huge stump. I could not resist the urge, so I crawled up on the stump, cupped my hands to my mouth and shouted as loud as I could in Joe's direction, "You S.O.B. you'll get it tomorrow; Gabe Meadow is going to be here."

Even as I shouted the words, doubt swept my mind. Could it be that I gave Gabe Meadow more credit than he deserved. We'd see. It was almost noon when I reached camp. Gabe had killed a nice three-year-old gobbler. I related as best I could all of the events of the morning and Gabe listened to every word. I knew Gabe didn't like to hunt during the afternoon in territory where he would be after a gobbling turkey the next morning. That suited me fine because I had enough of Joe to last for a while.

The next morning Gabe and I parted to hunt our assigned areas. How I hoped Gabe would bag old Joe and end this frustrating ordeal. When Gabe returned to camp about noon empty handed, Mr. Gallberry Joe began to weight my mind. Gabe didn't elaborate on his encounter with Joe in any great detail. He told me part of it and bragged on Joe by calling him "good turkey." Where I had worked myself up to a lather fretting about my inability to conquer Joe, Gabe was showing his appreciation of this turkey for offering us the opportunity of the encounter.

The uncertainty of the pursuit is the thing that keeps turkey hunting the greatest of all gun sports. Gabe once told me how he hunted certain character turkeys to a point of being reluctant to kill them after they furnished such great sport to him. Also, these great trophy and wise gobblers should be left to pass on to future generations of wild turkeys their genes and their traits.

I realized that I was a long way from this position on turkeys, as here I was, wishing all kinds of bad things would befall Gallberry Joe. Well, you live and learn, and I have hopes still of reaching this plateau of thinking relative to the wild turkey.

The third day of our stay in Lane County and my time to hunt Gallberry Joe arrived. That morning when Gallberry Joe answered my owling with gusto and what sounded like enthusiasm, I thought of what Mr. Tony McCleb had said. This durn turkey could hardly wait to lock horns with me or so it seemed. One thing for certain, he was probably more pleased with the set-up than I was. Again like Mr. Tony had said, Gallberry Joe maneuvered me into a game of checkers with him.

As explained earlier, the area resembled a giant checker board with patches of gallberry bushes and patches of grazed grass running between. Every time Gallberry Joe would move, I would change position. It was my hope somehow, Joe would make a mistake and move into the range of my gun which I held in firing position at each stand until my arms would almost drop off. More of Mr. Tony's sayings traveled through my mind— how he had played this game of checkers with turkeys in this gallberry jungle for days at a time, always without success. The other saying of Mr. Tony that someone would come along with a new trick and perhaps that would be what it took to get Gallberry Joe. I had turned this over in my mind hundreds of times, something new and different to try on Gallberry Joe.

This morning Joe was giving me the works. When I would yelp to Joe, he would answer with a gobble and come straight toward me, gobbling every thirty seconds. When he would reach a point about seventy-five yards away, all sounds would stop and for the next thirty minutes an eerie silence would prevail. There I would sit, gun raised, hammer back, watching for Gallberry Joe. My mind ran wild—what was he doing? Slipping up on me? Just standing there? Not knowing what else to do, I sat there until my arms ached. Finally I relaxed and lowered my gun. The next sound would be a lusty gobble from Joe at a point about two hundred yards from where I last heard him. This routine continued for several hours.

I knew there was a chance Gallberry Joe would make a

mistake. A very slim chance, I realized. Suddenly it struck me, an idea that might work. I got up and quietly made my way to the old logging road. When I reached the road, I yelped and cackled. Joe liked it and gobbled and started toward me as usual. Instead of sitting and waiting for Joe, I walked very rapidly down the old road away from Joe, yelping about each twenty-five steps. I was moving away from Joe and speeded up so I could get completely out of his hearing. Still I yelped and he was answering until I could not hear him anymore. I had moved completely out of his hearing. I figured I had moved about four or five hundred yards down the old road on top of the ridge. At this point I turned around and ran as fast as I could about two hundred yards back toward Gallberry Joe. I quickly selected a place about fifteen yards off the road and sat down in front of a large pine. Almost directly in front of me was a small opening that gave a pretty good view of about a ten-yard section of the old road.

I had hardly got seated before I saw the bobbing head of a turkey gobbler coming down the road. I followed this head with my 20-gauge single-barrel as the head of the turkey came in view and bobbed in and out of sight as he passed the gallberry bushes. He would shortly come completely in view when he got to the opening and I would have to make the best of it. Suddenly he burst into view—a sight to behold. He was a chesty, full-breasted, long-bearded turkey and the smallest I had ever seen to be so old. He was walking rapidly with his head held high. As he got into the opening I clucked to him and he stopped dead still. I believe he then realized his mistake, but at that time, I was squeezing the trigger of the 20-gauge. The saga of Gallberry Joe had ended.

It was a brisk, cool morning but sweat had popped out all over my body. I quickly had my foot on Joe's neck just below his head. He thrashed about fiercely and as life left him, I could see his spurs, fully an inch long, curved and sharp as a needle. Later in town at the butcher shop, we weighed Gallberry Joe—an unbelievable 13 lbs. 4 oz. Again old Tony Mc-Cleb had been right on target when he made the statement, ''He'll be about the size of that domineck rooster over there.''

Gallberry Joe was walking rapidly with his head held high.

I sat down by the side of Gallberry Joe for several minutes trying to gain my composure. I was so overwhelmed by my
success that mixed emotions crowded my mind. Thoughts ran
wild but mostly they were of Gabe Meadow and how he would
react. In back of it all, there kept rising up in me a feeling of
sadness. I believe this sad feeling was brought about by the
sight of a gallant feathered king who, one second, was the acme
of poise, stamina, and beauty, only to become in the next
moment a heap of feathers and blood.

Gabe was waiting at the camp for me. He had already broken
camp and was ready to travel. As expected, Gabe didn't really
make a big fuss over my feat. He acted like I had only done
what was expected of me. I wanted to tell Gabe the whole
story. It was always good to tell him anything because he
always made a super listener. We were headed home and I
knew stops would be made at Tony McCleb's and the town of
Daleboro. We were almost to Mr. Tony's house when I finished my story and Gabe made his comment. "Boy, you hit on
a good trick and one which hasn't been wore out by every person who calls himself a turkey hunter. In the spring when wild
turkey hens start nesting, laying, and setting, they do all kinds
of strange and unusual things. Sort of like a woman acts when
she is pregnant. One of the strange things these turkey hens do
is to start running about like they have become possessed of the
devil. They will yelp, cackle, and fuss about after flying down
in the morning and the boss gobbler will probably join them.
All of a sudden, the hens will start running like mad. The gobbler will try to follow and the hens will scatter, each to go their
separate way to the utter frustration of Mr. Gobbler. It's quite
simple, the hens don't want the gobbler around when they establish their nesting site. Nature makes the hen drab in color to
aid her in being able to hide herself as she sits on her nest.
She don't want Mr. Glamor standing around in his colorful at-
tire advertising the nesting site and generally making a nuisance
of himself. Now this is a bitter pill for the gobbler to swallow.
After months of strutting around being admired by these hens,
he suddenly becomes an unwanted cast aside. The gobbler does
his best to pursue these hens. When you suddenly up and

started rapidly away from Joe, he thought for sure this was a real hen because he had never had a hunter do this way."

I didn't tell Gabe that my trick was a pure accident but I suspected he knew it. Then and there I realized that, to become a complete turkey hunter, you need to learn all you can about a gobbler and his actions. Too, you need to learn all you can about the female and her actions and reactions.

When we reached Tony McCleb's house and showed him Gallberry Joe, it was something to see. One would have thought Tony had never seen a wild turkey before. Tony examined Gallberry Joe, making comments about the size of his spurs and beard and all this on so small a turkey. One thing kind of puzzled me because none of the people, including Mr. Tony, ever questioned that this turkey was Gallberry Joe. Mr. Tony kind of propped Gallberry Joe against a post on the porch and then Tony began to cluck and gobble and march around in the yard doing kind of a shuffling jig. Tony was working his hands at his side to imitate the wings of a strutting turkey. Suddenly Tony stopped this ceremony and began to lecture Gallberry Joe, censuring him, for letting a mere boy end what had been a promising career. Tony said to Gabe and me, "Take this turkey to Daleboro and put him on display. The whole town will want to see him. It will make some folks sad and some glad. You wouldn't believe what that little old turkey has done to the folks in that town and the surrounding countryside. Them who ain't hunting Joe is talking about him. Maybe now some gardens will get planted, houses patched up, fences mended, and the whole durn place will return to normal."

After my encounter with Gallberry Joe, I slowly began to realize for the first time what real turkey hunting was all about. After more than half a century of hunting the wild turkey, I am now coming to the realization that the classic challenging method of hunting the wild turkey is fast disappearing. I believe it probably took a thousand turkey gobbler candidates to produce a Gallberry Joe. How is a Gallberry Joe going to emerge when a novice can legally pick off even the most likely candidate with a scoped rifle at three hundred yards as he crosses a powerline right-of-way. Adding insult to tragedy, the novice will then drag the mutilated carcass of this turkey around bragging, "the turkey hunter would have you believe this bird is tough."

Almost as bad, but not quite, is the food plot hunting fraternity. They clear these open plots in wooded turkey habitat and plant them with foods irresistible to a wild turkey—chuffas, oats, wheat, clover, etc. They construct comfortable little houses at the plots' edges. Some of these fixed blinds or plot houses are downright elaborate, equipped with refreshments, carpeted floors, heaters, and easy chairs. On this stage now arrives the two main actors, the turkey and the hunter, both hell-bent to follow the course of least resistance: the turkey, to gather his food with the least effort; and the hunter, to bag the turkey with ease and in real comfort. Here again, a good turkey gobbler is easy to take by anyone who can pull the trigger of a gun and shoot in the general direction of the turkey. What a difference in this and the classical method of hunting which is clearly described in this book. In chapter 11 of this book, you will find an attempt to put the different methods and ways to turkey hunt in their true perspective.

5

Tony McCleb

ONE of the most fascinating things about turkey hunting is the
fact that no matter how many years you hunt the turkey, you
will not be bored. No two seasons will be alike, no two turkeys
will be alike, and when you throw in the people characters who
hunt turkeys and you associate with, it makes for one grand
melee.

Mr. Tony McCleb of Lane County, I believe, was one of the
most unique characters who ever lived to become a kind of
patriarch of all turkey hunters. Tony's background placed him
in a position of undisputed knowledge and wisdom of all things
concerning the wild turkey. He came from a family who for
generations were famous turkey hunters. He came from an area
where the wild turkey had survived in sufficient quantities to be
hunted every single year that the white man had lived here. Of
course, prior to the arrival of the white man, Tony's area was
the choice hunting ground of the Indian, due to its abundance of
game, particularly the wild turkey. Thus Tony McCleb became a
kind of clearing house of information for turkey hunters.

When people began to make turkey calls to sell on the market, Tony became the unofficial tester of many of these calls.
It was very important to the maker of turkey calls to have Mr.
Tony hear the call and comment on it. Now Tony was known for
his candid opinions and caustic comments. One fellow I knew
told me he had worked on a certain kind of call for years to perfect it. He was about ready to market it and decided to go over

to Lane County and get Tony McCleb's opinion of the call. He
said to Tony, "Mr. Tony, I want you to listen to this call and
tell me frankly what you would do if you was a turkey gobbler
and heard these sounds." The call-maker said he then pro-
ceeded to give forth with what he considered the sweetest turkey
sounds ever to come from a turkey call. Old Tony cocked his
head to listen and, after having heard, quickly gave the man his
verdict. "Son, if I was a gobbler and heard that sound, I'd run
like hell—away from it." The call maker said he thanked Mr.
Tony and decided then and there that he would not try to make
or market the call.

Tony said one day he was sitting on a bench in front of a
store in Daleboro, when a nice-looking teenage boy came up to
him. The boy said to Tony, "Mr. Tony, will you help me? I
have been taking a lot of ribbing about something that happened. I don't know what to believe or what to do." Without
hesitation, Tony said, "Lay it out to me, boy. I'll do what I
can." The boy said he went with his older brother to a turkey
camp over in Alabama. A bunch of turkey hunters were at this
camp and there were some who seemed to have come to pick at
the hunters instead of hunting themselves.

"Anyhow," continued the boy, "a big rainstorm came before
daylight one morning and continued till about eight o'clock.
When the rain suddenly quit, all the hunters scattered to the
woods to hunt. It so happened, as I was walking down this old
logging road, a Mr. Tate from Birmingham caught up with me
and we were walking and talking. Suddenly we came across a
set of turkey tracks which crossed the road. These tracks must
have been made by the boss gobbler of those parts. They were
big and the turkey who made them must have been awful heavy,
as the tracks sank deep in the mud. I was the first to discover
the tracks and called Mr. Tate's attention to them," said the
boy. "I said to Mr. Tate: Look, Mr. Tate, at these tracks.
They couldn't have been made more than five minutes ago and
this old turkey went right down this hollow." The boy said Mr.
Tate backed up a little and said, "Boy, don't you know that a
big old wise turkey gobbler don't just walk across a road. He is
too smart for that. When he comes to a road or path, he care-

fully backs across it to throw off some folks who don't know no better." The boy then said to Tony, "Mr. Tony, I know you will tell me the truth about this. Some folks say it is so and others say it ain't. All of them seem to get a big kick out of confusing me."

If there was a soft spot in Tony McCleb's heart, it would be for young turkey hunters. It miffed Tony to hear folks picking at these young hunters. I have heard him say, "Why poke fun at a young turkey hunter? A boy who starts turkey hunting don't need obstacles strewed in his path by people. Turkeys will do that. What the boy needs is understanding." Tony said to the boy, "Son, there is no wild critter in this world who has sense enough to back across a road to confuse a hunter. Anyway, a wild turkey don't need to do that—there is not one hunter in a thousand who can follow a turkey gobbler in the woods and get up with him." Tony continued, "Let me tell you something else. Don't you let any of these so called turkey hunters pick you for information on turkeys you have located. Some of these people are past masters at doing just that. They will let someone do the footwork to locate turkeys and then pick it out of the locator for their own advantage. These old rogues know young people will tell them the truth about where they saw turkeys. On the other hand, old hunters will either tell a downright lie or will be so vague, their information would be worthless. When you have hunted turkeys for eight or ten years, you will learn to protect your hard-won secrets and information. It is not a matter of being selfish; it is a matter of protecting something that belongs to you. Kinda like putting money in the bank."

Tony said this young boy just kind of caught his fancy as a good potential turkey man. Tony said to this boy, "Why don't you come over and spend the day with me sometime? I'll show you some tricks and give you some advice that will help you. If you are going to be a turkey hunter, you'll need all the help you can get. You know what, I really believe wild turkeys are getting smarter and smarter. Their ability to adapt to changes has meant the difference in turkeys surviving or going out of the picture. Why, back in Indian days when a turkey flew up in the top of a real tall tree, he was safe. There was no way an Indian could kill him. Now you know no turkey is going to sit up in a tree and let you walk up with a gun and shoot him. Just the other day, I was down in my pasture sitting under a big sweetgum tree and I saw this drove of turkeys feeding along the edge of the pasture. There was three old hens and fifteen young turkeys. I'd say the young ones were about two-thirds grown and you could already tell the gobblers from the hens by their looks. Then too, you could tell the gobblers from the hens by the way they acted and carried themselves. There at the pasture's edge were a few scattered small pine trees about the size of your wrist. Every time the drove of turkeys would get close to this patch of small pine trees, every last one of the six young gobblers would run over to these pine trees and stand straight up by them. It was the dernest thing you ever saw, as they seemed to melt into them very small trees. Now what do you think these young gobblers were doing? Practicing, that's what. Only the gobblers were doing this practicing. It was something to see. Here comes along fifteen young turkeys and, before you know it, there are only nine—six have evaporated.''

Tony watched the boy carefully to see if he was getting any-thing out of turkey talk being beamed at him. Obviously the boy was enjoying it, because Tony continued. ''You know by looking at a turkey that he is well-built to look around a tree; his eyes kind of stand out and he can peep around objects without exposing himself. A man is different—if he tries to peep around a tree, he exposes too much of himself before his eyes can see. When you hunt turkeys, don't ever get behind a tree, it is bet-ter to get in front of it, sit down and be still.''

Tony was getting warmed up. ''Once when the season was in, I was crossing the pasture to hunt the woods on the other side. I usually crossed at the ends of the oblong pasture to take advantage of the cover it afforded. I was about half way across the pasture and stopped by this bush to look over the pasture. As if by magic, there—way down in the other end of the pasture —stood this big gobbler. Of course, I froze and watched as the gobbler began to strut. The turkey was putting on quite a show trying to attract some females to come over and consort with him. After strutting around in little circles with his wattles red as fire, the turkey would stand tall to see if any company was coming. Of course, always on his mind were his enemies, and he watched constantly for them. A slight breeze was blowing from where the turkey was toward me. I knew I would not be able to make this turkey hear my call. The pasture had cows and calves scattered about and some were between me and the turkey. I figured if I could ease down the side of the pasture, staying next to the woods, and get to a point about half way to the turkey, I could make the turkey hear my call.

"I had two things which I knew were in my favor. First, was the breeze blowing. When you want to move around in turkey country, watch for breezes which often will be blowing in gusts. When you see grass and trees moving from the breezes, that's when you move. The second thing was the turkey strutting around in circles. When he has his back to you and his fan fully opened, he can't see you, so you can move a few steps. So crouching low, I was making good progress toward my goal. Every time the turkey turned his back, I moved up a little and would stop before he turned around facing me. The breeze was helping me. When lots of movement is going on, a turkey can't pick up a single movement as well as when the air is still. I was kind of figuring when the turkey would turn around and at one point, figured wrong. The turkey turned and caught me in the act of moving. He snapped to attention, adjusted his wings and I believe was going to take off. I was caught red handed but a quick thought raced through my mind and I let out a couple of bleats like a calf, 'M-a-a-a-a, M-a-a-a.' Would you believe that durn turkey accepted me as a calf, because he relaxed and started strutting again.

"I have hunted and watched turkeys enough to know they get suspicious of objects and movements and are often unduly alarmed. They frequently find out their suspicions are not founded and they quickly accept that and return to normal. I had to slow down my movements after that, because the gobbler was now suspicious and probably would not put up with any other thing that was out of the ordinary. Finally I got to a place I felt would be all right to make my stand. I sat in front of a big pine just off the edge of the pasture. Some bushes were between me and the pasture and that was all right since I could see between them. The turkey was standing looking toward the other side of the pasture, when I gave him my five fast mating call yelps on my box. When these sweet sounds reached the turkey, I saw his head turn just a little bit to catch all the sounds. The turkey was an old one and showed no emotion but again started his strut, stop, and look routine. He was of course hoping the hen would run down the pasture to him. He would look longingly in my direction for her. I never uttered another sound, just sat and watched. You don't get to see the full show like this often. When you do, take advantage of all you see, because this experience is worth a lot to you. After about fifteen minutes the gobbler started slowly in my direction. He approached with extreme caution and I was glad I had a good place to sit to him. When he finally got in range, I squeezed the trigger of my double 12-gauge and the turkey was mine. I examined the turkey carefully and believe he was an Alabama turkey. The Alabama line is about ten miles east of here as the crow flies. This four-year-old turkey had obviously fought his way through the territories of lots of old gobblers. His legs showed lots of scarred places and his wings were ragged and worn. Son, this turkey was what us old turkey hunters call a running turkey.

"At certain times in the spring, a few of the unattached gobblers—this is, gobblers without harems—will take off on a wild spree. The gobbler may make a circuit of twenty miles or more. Now, Boy, old Mama Nature did a masterful job in making the wild turkey in the first place. In close second place was the masterful way that she inbred in the wild turkey certain traits that helps carry on the breed. This trait of vigorous gobblers running all over the country, double checking all females to see that they are mated to carry on the race, is something to behold. You know it ain't easy for a gobbler to travel unfamiliar territories, roosting in strange places and running up against jealous old gobblers who fight to protect their females. Not all gobblers take up this running routine, only the adventuresome ones ever do it.

"Now, these running gobblers are by far the easiest of all

Mature gobblers often travel in droves.

The turkey decided to try to intimidate the calf ~ but lost the battle.

turkeys to kill. He gets downright lonesome for any turkey who will take up some time with him. The gobblers he meets want to fight. Most of the females he meets completely ignore him. So it is just natural when some hen beams a little love song in his direction, he's for sure going to get up with her.'' Tony was really giving this boy a baptism of turkey talk. Tony continued. ''Some of these lazy hunters will only hunt when turkey gobblers are running. That's like fishing only when bream are on the beds.''

Tony noted the boy was all tensed up and the seriousness of Tony's turkey talk brought on a somber mood. Tony would up his turkey talk with a lighter story, as he said, ''Perhaps you think all turkey talk and turkey hunting has to be cold serious. That ain't necessarily so because there are plenty of clowns of nature out there to amuse you. At times I have had wild turkeys entertain me with some good clown acts. A year or so ago, I saw this two-year-old gobbler and a three-month-old calf put on a mock fight that would have tickled your ribs. Most times a turkey gobbler is scared of everything including his own shadow. I have seen all kinds of birds and small animals run a gobbler away from an area. Now this two-year-old gobbler was picking clover in the pasture when up comes this nosy three-month-old calf. Ordinarily the turkey would take off, but not this one. The turkey decided he would try to intimidate the calf. The turkey would drop his wings to the ground and puff up like in a strut and run at the calf. The calf would watch and suddenly would run to meet the turkey at which point the turkey would turn tail and run like the devil. This went on for fully an hour. After running off a couple hundred yards, the turkey would take heart and again come to try to scare the calf, with wings spread out full length. Sometimes the turkey would beat his wings fiercely and hop around the calf pecking at him. The calf never gave an inch and according to my verdict was the undisputed winner of the fray.''

With this lighter-toned tale, Tony took leave of the boy but not before finding out if he had answered the boy's questions satisfactorily. If a hunter carefully followed Tony's stories, he could always pick up valuable tips on turkey hunting. Tony was a past master at concealing them in his colorful stories.

6

Tony McCleb's Secret

GABE MEADOW and I were laying plans for the upcoming spring turkey season. We would hunt in both Alabama and Mississippi as was our custom. Alabama usually opened the spring turkey season seven to ten days before Mississippi. As Gabe said, this gives you a chance to get a little of the wild out of your system and settle to real hunting.

When you hunt the same area year after year, very little preseason scouting is desirable. Perhaps one or two short trips to see that the turkeys are there and no major change has been made in the physical makeup of the area, is o.k. Gabe and I agreed on this point. When turkeys see a sudden increase of activity in an area, they sense hunting pressure is about to begin and may leave the locality or hole up in the thickets. If, however, you are going to hunt new territory, scouting is a must.

Our preparation for the season was mostly getting in the mood, which wasn't really hard to do. Simple turkey talk usually did the trick. I loved these jam sessions with Gabe as I was still learning from this old master. It was a good time to check out some event or an act of a turkey which puzzled me.

More than once I had a turkey pull the following tricks on me. I was sitting back from this pretty hollow, just far enough to see about one-quarter mile down it. It was mid-morning and about every fifteen minutes I would yelp. Big timber covered the hollow and you could see a long way. After a while I saw a

turkey making his way up the hollow toward me. I believe he
had heard my yelping because every now and then he would
stop and carefully eye the area where I was. The course he was
taking carried him to the right of me as he came up out of the
hollow. He was about eighty yards away and now on about the
same level with me. For a few minutes he stood there, and I
dared not move a muscle. Slowly he turned and started walking
toward a huge stump which was about twenty-five yards directly
in front of me. Nonchalantly he moved toward the stump and
once or twice stopped to pick at something on the ground. I figured he was going to walk behind the stump and that would
give me the chance to ease my gun in position. He did walk behind the stump, and I raised my gun and waited for him to step
out on the other side. There I sat, gun aimed and every minute
expecting the turkey to step out and get killed. Time moved
slowly and my arms grew heavy. I waited and waited—no turkey. From my position I thought I could see both sides of the
stump and the area beyond the stump. Tension and fatigue was
taking its toll and I knew I couldn't keep this up very long. I
stood it as long as I could and would have wagered any amount,
the turkey was still behind the stump. I decided my only chance
was to jump up and charge the stump, and that's what I did.
To my utter amazement, there was no turkey there. I couldn't
believe it. I even looked carefully around the stump for a hole
the turkey could have crawled into. No hole. A turkey hunter
has to learn to accept things he doesn't understand. I sure
didn't understand what had just happened but I had to accept it.
	Several years passed when almost an exact rerun of this
"turkey-behind-stump" routine took place. I was hunting an
area in West Alabama. It was up in the day and I was sitting
relaxed on the edge of a big swamp. I had been yelping at intervals but truthfully had little faith in calling up a turkey in that
particular location. Very few turkey signs were evident and I
was mostly just enjoying the warm sun after being cold all
morning. I suddenly realized that a big gobbler was standing
off to my left, not more than sixty yards away. He was staring
at me but showed no sign that he recognized me. My gun lay
across my lap, a hopeless situation. To my amazement, the

turkey started moving along the edge of the swamp, not directly toward me, but angling in my direction. He was picking and at times scratching his way slowly along. It dawned on me then that this turkey was going to try to pull the vanishing act on me. I studied this turkey intently and the only thing he did out of the ordinary was to lift his wings a few inches above his back and then again position them on his back. His course would bring him within twenty-five yards of where I sat. I then noticed a patch of blackberry vines with half grown leaves directly in front of me. The turkey walked behind this thin cover, I raised my gun, and another vanishing turkey act took place right before my eyes. To make matters worse, I was looking for it to happen, tried to prevent it from happening, and was now more amazed than the first time this trick was played on me. As with the first time, this trick was played and I was the loser.

I then went up and checked the scene carefully. I went to the point where I saw the turkey the first time, retraced his route to the point behind the blackberry vines, and studied the spot where I was sitting when it all took place. How he could walk up this close to me and use this thin cover to simply walk away from me, I cannot understand. I even found his tracks behind the blackberry vines. The moist soft earth at the swamp's edge told the whole story in turkey tracks. This big gobbler made big tracks and a big impression on me. Two days later I evened the score with him. I flushed his harem of hens away from him at dawn and sat down to call him quite easily to my gun. His fine beard and feet with a long sharp set of spurs are among my collection. It is almost sad that a turkey as smart as this one would have some small flaw in his armor and thus permit someone to take his life. He simply had learned to put too much dependence in the hens who usually protected him.

I wanted to talk to Gabe about these tricks of turkeys which so amazed me. Gabe listened attentively as I told him of the two times turkeys pulled this vanishing act on me. I detailed the events as closely as I could and deliberately left out only one part. The way each one of these turkeys raised their wings slightly and kind of adjusted them on their backs. Gabe was well pleased that I had recognized the maneuvers of these turkeys as deliberate defensive acts. Gabe said this maneuver had saved the lives of a lot of turkeys. He noted that only old turkeys would try it.

Gabe said, "Some folks say turkeys are not able to think. This act alone proves not only can a turkey think but he does it to a very high degree. Now you think about it. He walks up to a point, say seventy-five yards away, where he sees a man. At that point, he doesn't have the cover to walk away from the man without being seen. He quickly sizes up his options. He sees this clump of bushes or a big tree or stump. He knows by getting that cover between him and the man, he can simply slip away from the man, unseen. He pretends that he doesn't see the man. That's smart. He even nonchalantly picks and scratches his way to the cover. That's smart. He is moving closer and closer to the man convincing the man hat he hasn't seen him. That takes guts and brains. I have had them walk within fifteen feet of me during this maneuver. One of the wild turkey's greatest talents is to get a small object between him and his hunter and walk away without being visible at any time. One of my greatest joys in turkey hunting is to have a big old gobbler go through this maneuver, putting on his act with finesse and precision. I am sure people who hunt turkeys a great deal have turkeys pull this trick on them but you won't have many hunters talk about it. I don't believe most of these hunters ever really realize this great maneuver as a deliberate act; rather they view it as a kind of accident. One point I would make with you here. When you believe a turkey is trying to pull this trick on you, take very careful note of every move he makes. If at some point the turkey raises his wings a little way off his back and then kind of adjusts them and lays them back down, look out; he's for sure going to pull the trick. Fact is, anytime you see a gobbler do this, he sees you or thinks he does. This wing adjusting bit is a dead give away. You know, of course, that he is rightfully proud of those powerful wings. They make the difference in their being wild turkeys or not being wild turkeys. When this gobbler sees you, he just has to be sure his wings are still there. So he moves them a little to assure himself. Kind of like Wyatt Earp would do. Wyatt

He is deciding the route to take - try to influence him, now.

Tony McCleb's house with dog trot or hall through the middle.

always had his guns on him, but when he saw a tight spot coming up, he just naturally had to feel his guns to make sure.''

Over the fifty-three years I have hunted turkeys, I have had six turkeys pull this trick on me. When they did it, I never killed a one of them. Like Gabe said, I always got a big kick out of it, and any man who hunts turkeys should look for this great turkey maneuver. It will fascinate you as it has Gabe and me.

Along about this time, Gabe took a hankering to go down to Lane County and talk with Tony McCleb. I got the impression that Mr. Tony wasn't doing too good health-wise. Someone from Lane County gave a message to Gabe that Mr. Tony McCleb wanted to have a talk with him. Out of the great respect Gabe had for Tony, we took off in Gabe's old pickup truck for the domain of Tony McCleb.

Several years had passed since I had seen Mr. Tony. Matter of fact, the last time I saw him was the spring I killed that famous Lane County turkey, Gallberry Joe. That was five years ago, which would make Tony McCleb ninety-five years old. Gabe and I camped the same place we camped when hunting Gallberry Joe. The familiar surroundings brought back the memories of that eventful trip.

When we arrived at Tony McCleb's house, it did my heart good to see how glad Tony was to see us. Country folks get lonesome at times and good company didn't come by every day or every week for that matter. Gabe said to Tony, "Mr. Tony, the boy and me are going to be down this way for several days. If it is all right with you, we'll come over every morning we are here to visit with you." Mr. Tony, of course, agreed with that and came quickly to the point of telling Gabe why he had sent word that he wanted to see him. Tony said he realized his life was winding down and it was his hope that he could have one good long visit with Gabe before the end came. "I want to do some turkey talking with you, Gabe Meadow," said Tony.

I could tell that Tony McCleb had aged some. However, for his age, he was still a remarkable man. He and Gabe talked for about three hours each morning and I listened. If I could have recorded this last series of talks between Gabe Meadow and Tony McCleb, that recording would be my most prized possession. Tony may have slipped physically but certainly not mentally. Like a master host, he would frequently beam a tale in my direction. We were sitting on the porch one day when two of the many roosters on the place squared off for a fight. We all watched with interest and it reminded Tony of one of his childhood pranks. Tony said once he had a neighbor boy come over to spend a few days with him. The visiting boy was amazed at the number of roosters on the McCleb place and by the fact they hardly ever fought each other. Tony explained that the roosters had a pecking order—each knew the roosters who could whip him and the roosters he could whip. Tony said he had often figured on how to change the pecking order and start these roosters fighting. One day he figured a way but had not had a chance to try it. Perhaps now would be a good time. The whole McCleb chicken flock was a colorful sight. Every size and color you can imagine. Lots of white, red, black, yellow, and mixed colors. Tony and his boy guest slipped some corn out of the crib, some soot from the chimney, and some flour from the barrel in the pantry. With the corn, they caught every white and black rooster on the place. The black ones they covered with flour and the white ones they covered with soot. Tony said every rooster on the place became involved in a free-for-all. Roosters fought for three days. Tony said after about one day, his mama and papa joined the fight, having found out about Tony's prank. Tony said his Ma and Pa used up three plum bushes of switches on him and his friend. For the benefit of the "now" generation, it was customary in Tony's day for the host parents to discipline any "youngun" who might be under their roof.

The time had come for Gabe and me to go home. Gabe told Tony at the beginning of the last morning session we would be leaving that day.

When Gabe announced that we were going home, a kind of eerie silence fell on our group. For a short time nothing was said and that was unusual around Tony McCleb. In a few minutes, Tony arose slowly from his huge rocking chair and said,

"Let's take a walk down the road a piece." Gabe and I followed as Tony carefully and slowly led us down the narrow road to a point overlooking the entire valley of the beautiful Buckatuna River. There by the road stood one of the largest white oak trees I ever saw. Tony sat down and leaned against this huge tree and indicated for Gabe and me to do the same. From our vantage point, the green valley of the Buckatuna River wound its way southward. The valley was completely covered with timber —hardwood along the river, pine on the gentle slopes leading to the ridges. Tony said, "This here oak was here when I was a boy. Course t'was smaller then. I have leaned against it all these years, physically and mentally. When I get tired physically, I come here and sit and it rests me. When my mind is disturbed or I need to do some thinking, I come and sit and my mind soon gets settled. The peace of the valley seems to come up here better than any other place I know." After a few more minutes of small talk, Tony's mood changed to one of austere seriousness.

"Gabe," Tony said, "I have known you for many, many years. You are the most dedicated wild turkey man I ever knew. The fact that you have taken this boy [me] under your wing, speaks well of him. I have decided to share a secret with you two which has been closely guarded by the McCleb clan for generations and generations. More than eight generations have passed it down. As you know, me and my cousins, Deak and Zeke, are the last of the McClebs. I don't have any boys to pass the secret to. It wouldn't do to turn the secret over to Deak and Zeke, that's for sure. Now y'all just settle back and listen careful to what I am going to tell you." You could tell that Tony had wrestled with this decision-making for some time and now that he had resolved it, he was at peace.

Tony McCleb's eye sparkled with enthusiasm as he began to lay out this remarkable story. He said, "I don't have to tell you what an outlandish creature a wild turkey really is. In all this world there is no creature that comes close to being what a wild turkey is. Because a wild turkey is so different, it takes a special breed of men to deal with him and to appreciate him. Then out of this special breed of men, a few rise above the rest to

become what I call 'turkey men.' Now you turkey men listen
to this.''

Tony laid it out with quiet, convincing tones. "The most curious creature on this earth is a monkey. The next most curious
is a wild turkey. Remember that. If a turkey sees a man, he
leaves in a hurry. If a turkey sees or hears a dog, he does the
same. He instantly recognizes by sight and sound all of his
enemies. The fox or the bobcat will half scare him out of his
wits and he quickly runs or flies from them. But if a wild turkey sees something he has never seen before, his overpowering
curiosity gets a hold of him, simply paralyzes him with the desire to find out what the unfamiliar thing is. He will hold his
ground as this new thing approaches, hoping to find out what it
is. Only a turkey man is going to believe what I am now going
to tell y'all. You run into this old turkey who won't come to
you, and everything else in your bag of tricks fails. Others as
well as you have failed to kill him and it seems he is not to be
had. He may be invincible to all others but not to the men who
possess the McCleb secret. This old turkey is out there and you
are going to get him. Here is how. After you locate him, stop
right there and start taking off your clothes. Take off every
stitch, even your hat, your shoes, and socks. Get just as naked
as the day you came into this world. Now get down on your all
fours, that is your hands and knees, and start backing toward
the turkey. If you do it right, the turkey will be so paralyzed
with curiosity at the sight you present to him, he just ain't going
to run or fly. He's got to find out what it is. He may walk
around in small circles clucking, but he ain't going nowhere.
Boys, take my word for it. This trick works. McClebs have
used it for generations and it helped earn for all of them great
reputations. I have used it. Now guard it careful and use it
only when you have to.''

When Tony McCleb finished this episode, he sat back with
eyes closed. Seems like he wanted us to take the time to let his
secret soak in. I have never seen Gabe in quite the state of
confusion he was in now. He didn't know what to say. Whether to thank Tony or not; whether to accept this secret as a gift

or as an amusing anecdote. Of course, it completely flabbergasted me.

The talk turned to other subjects as we made our way back to Tony's house. Never once did Tony mention the secret again. When we got ready to go, Tony thanked us for our visits and talks.

Would you believe that to this day, Gabe Meadow has never mentioned the Tony McCleb secret. Mr. Tony said the monkey holds first place as the most curious creature. In second place is the wild turkey. At that time, in third place went Gene Nunnery. I earned that place due to the great degree of curiosity I had to find out what Gabe thought about Tony's secret. I have had to live over forty years with this secret gnawing at my curiosity. If Gabe had just given me his opinion, it would have eased my mind. Foxy old Tony McCleb knew how to be remembered. His love for entertaining goes on even after his life has passed.

Was this Tony McCleb secret one big joke? Was it, in fact, a true and normal tactic that would work on a turkey? I have pondered these facts and am now just as uncertain about the entire matter as I was the day Tony McCleb stunned Gabe and me with it. I know for a fact that wild turkeys have great curiosities. I know, also, that their reaction to any situation is most unpredictable. As I have said before, I will believe almost anything a person tells me about a wild turkey. On several occasions, I have been tempted to try the Tony McCleb secret. I may try it yet. Anyway I feel a lot better about it, since sharing this secret with you. It helps some to have others ponder this turkey tale for what it is worth.

Three turkeys

7

The Phantom of Possum Creek

IN East Mississippi there is a very special little creek. For the last six or eight miles of its course, it turns and runs due north and right past the place where I was born. This running north is exactly opposite to the general direction of the flow of other streams, as they all flow in a southerly direction.

On the opposite side of the creek from my birthplace was Lauderdale Springs. From these famous springs there flowed water of several different chemical constituents—iron, sulphur, alum, and others—making the springs unique. My family hauled water from the springs to drink. When we would go after this water, my mother would have all us kids wade in the little rivulets running from the springs on their way to Possum Creek. Our bare feet were thus treated to the medicinal value of this water to help heal the many cuts and abrasions always present on a country boy's feet.

Legend has it that these springs were sacred to the native Indian before the coming of the white man. The Indians called them "The Healing Springs." When the Indian learned they would be moved from the area through the edicts of a treaty, "The Treaty of Dancing Rabbit Creek," the Indian was upset to leave their springs. They decided to make a huge earthen pot with which to cover the healing springs to hide them. They then dug and constructed an underground ditch to carry and conceal the flow from the springs and to run it into Possum Creek. Further up the creek from my birthplace there was an Indian burial mound. My father and I would go up and sit on top of this mound when I was a small boy. My father knew the Indian and was no novice when it came to spinning a yarn about them.

Today almost at the site of the Indian mound, a huge dam impounds the water of Possum Creek. The lake, I understand, is one of the largest privately owned lakes in the world.

Now, why all this information about Possum Creek? The reason for so much of a buildup is to lend emphasis to a character who is about to come on the scene. The character, a durn turkey gobbler I named "The Phantom of Possum Creek."

Several years had passed since I killed Gallberry Joe in Lane County. During these years I was enjoying a run of good luck in my turkey hunting. This luck, I believe, was partly brought about because I had learned to be aggressive when hunting a turkey gobbler. I was basking in the wake of my success. Also, I had gained somewhat of a reputation, which I sought to justify by killing several good turkeys each year.

Into this situation there came this turkey gobbler, "The Phantom of Possum Creek." I learned about the Phantom from a turkey that was whipping all hunters who challenged him. This friend started by asking me if I knew where Possum Creek was. I looked at my friend like a bull looking at a new gate. Man, would you believe I was born on this creek and during floods would have to raise my bed higher to keep out of Possum Creek?

Where the old Indian mound was and the huge lake now is, was Possum Creek swamp. This swamp was very flat and marshy. The palmetto grew all over this swamp in profusion. It was a primitive place and this durn phantom turkey had found out what a fine place it was to live. A good fringe benefit of living here was that you were entertained by folks who called themselves turkey hunters. When I went with my friend up to the Phantom's domain to look it over, it struck me—the similarity of this place to Gallberry Joe's range in Lane County. The palmetto replaced the gallberry bush. The palmettos grew in patches and cows grazed the narrow strips between—another checkerboard. One big difference. In Gallberry Joe's place, it was high and dry; but in the Phantom's domain, it was low, flat, and wet.

I have many good friends in this locality and I began to talk to them to get the Phantom's background. I found out that people hunted this turkey almost year round, in season and out. In fact, one man who worked for the owner of this area had built up such a desire to bag this turkey that it became kind of a local joke. The more the community rode this poor fellow as to the outcome of his hunts for the Phantom, the more this fellow strove to kill him. This man wasn't even a turkey hunter by name, but spent his time trying to bushwhack Mr. Phantom. When I came on the scene, I believe the bushwacker had about given up because he told me, "I don't believe anybody is going to kill that turkey. That damn turkey has got one and one half billion swamp mosquitoes, four hundred thousand big deer ticks, and several hundred snakes—including some of the biggest rat-tlesnakes and cottonmouth moccasins you ever saw—all working for him. These allies of his is as crazy as he is. Why them mosquitoes drinks insecticides, gets drunk off it, and would at-tack a bull elephant or a crocodile."

This Possum Creek turkey, unlike Gallberry Joe, was full sized, probably weighing a full eighteen pounds. This full breasted, long bearded turkey would gobble any time of day you came in contact with him, which led one to believe he was look-ing for a fight and, as Old Tony McCleb had said, enjoying it.

This first year I learned about the Phantom and began to hunt him was most enjoyable. The fact that I was returning to an area that I had rambled and explored as a child and boy held its own fascination. The more time I spent in this Possum Creek area, the more interesting it became as I recognized objects and things I had not seen for years and years. To put the icing on the cake, now there was a trophy turkey invading my old stomp-ing grounds and it would add to my prestige to take this turkey. I didn't continuously hunt the Phantom but would drop out and kill a good turkey or two in other places to kind of assure my-self that I could take any turkey that walked. It is true that I enjoyed my surroundings at Possum Creek so much that I prob-ably didn't pressure the Phantom to my full potential. This was at the first part of our engagement.

I hunted the Phantom for some time and he was taking all I put to him in stride. Trick after trick I played on him and not only did he survive, but he did it with arrogance. I even played the trick that caused the downfall of Gallberry Joe, to no avail. The realization was coming to me that this was no ordinary turkey. I had not told Gabe of my plans to hunt the Phantom. I thought I would run up to Possum Creek a few times, toy with this turkey, bag him, and then let Gabe know about it. It sure wasn't working out that way. Was this turkey going to bring me down to mingle again with the ordinary turkey hunters? I had heard Gabe say many times that every turkey hunter meets his match when he plays by the rules. At these times a man is put on trial to see if, in fact, he is a real turkey hunter. When a certain turkey whips and humbles a man, some men will weaken and resort to unfair tactics to kill the turkey. Actually, the turkey has done the man a great favor and the dumb man can't see it. Every time a turkey out-smarts a hunter, that turkey etches the details on the memory of that man. These memories remain stored away and available when needed. Think of old ninety-five-year-old Tony McCleb and the shelves of stored memories he must have. Don't you know that he can set up on his porch and hunt again and again. He can pull out of his memory a certain turkey and play the game over, changing an item of tactic here and there to try to still outdo Mr. Turkey. Now search the memory of any man to see what turkeys are there. The ones who are there are the ones who survived man's best efforts to kill them.

I would guess the mass of palmettos covered an area of a square mile. The Phantom spent most of his time in this palmetto jungle. Often he would roost at the edges but when you challenged him, he would hustle to his preferred area. One morning the Phantom was roosting on the side of a ridge overlooking the palmetto jungle. He gobbled at my owling and it was still dark enough to conceal me. Very quietly I made my way into the palmetto jungle. I intended to cut him off from it. I worked my way around him until I was in the place I wanted to be. This was a switch for the Phantom and me. He on the outside and me on the inside. I had switched turkey calls, which I often did when working the same turkey several times. I had practiced the little soft yelps and now presented them to the Phantom. He exploded with some of the durndest gobbling you ever heard. After yelping I had moved very quickly about forty yards and was determined to remain here indefinitely without making another sound. The stage was set and I felt good about my chances. I knew the Phantom was going to try to get back to his palmetto paradise, come hell or high water. After a while he flew down and started walking up and down the side of the ridge. He would gobble furiously for about five minutes; and then, for twenty or thirty minutes, total silence. As already stated, I intended not yelping again. Each of us was, in effect, giving the other the silent treatment. Cold war at its hottest. The Phantom didn't like it one bit and he would break his periods of silence with the most arrogant gobbling and screeching you ever heard. The screech of a wild turkey gobbler. Turkey gobblers don't make this sound often, and I have heard it only four or five times in my over fifty years of close contact with them. Maybe all of them don't know how to make this sound. It could be that only the ones possessed of the devil can screech at a man. The bushwacker had told me of the mosquito population and the hordes of ticks, and I believe he grossly understated their numbers. Swarms of big swamp mosquitoes had found me as I sat to the Phantom. They swarmed above my head and looked much like the black whirling funnel of a tornado. I know the Phantom knew about this whirling mass of allies and heartily approved of their aid.

It was now several hours since I had heard the first gobble from this Phantom. At least forty-five minutes had passed since I heard him the last time. I had not uttered a sound since my first series of soft yelps at dawn. I knew he wanted to get back into his palmetto sanctuary. Wouldn't it seem logical for him to believe that it was now safe to simply stroll down the ridge into the swamp?

There was a sizable herd of cattle in the area. As I watched the side of the ridge where I had last heard the Phantom, I saw a bunch of cows coming along a cow trail that wound its way along the side of the ridge. It was a real assortment of cows:

large cows, small cows, all sizes of calves and every one a different color. They marched single file along the trail which would later enter the swamp. I casually watched the colorful procession as it moved slowly along. I was careful though to keep the rest of the ridge under observation as I thought perhaps the Phantom might use this diversion to slip past me into the swamp. I would say at least twenty-five cows and calves were now in full view. No two alike in color or size, yet they all had the same rocking gait as they ambled along. Suddenly it struck me—not all of this procession was cows. For there wedged in the middle of the herd was the Phantom. Now read carefully. The Phantom was about middle way of the bunch. He was ambling along head held out front like a cow—eyes forward—and using the same rocking gait of the rest of the cows and calves. The fact that he had already passed right by me in easy gun range proves how well he imitated his friends, the cows.

Now, if I had never told a lie in my whole life, the fact that I have told this story over and over has earned me somewhat of a reputation of being careless with the truth. Several things I have learned from this event and its telling. There is no use at all in telling this story to the non-hunters, for you won't find one believer in the lot. The more experienced the turkey hunter is who hears the story, the more likely he will be a believer. Fact is, I believe anything a turkey hunter tells me about his relations and experiences with the wild turkey. In other words, I deem all turkey hunters truthful until proven otherwise.

I have had enough trouble come my way that I can recognize it instantly no matter what form it comes in. When the Phantom pulled this trick on me, I knew I was in deep trouble. I had badly underestimated this turkey, as you will agree as I continue to tell you about him.

It was now open warfare between the Phantom and me. No more fooling around, and I would use every trick I had to take the Phantom.

One fine morning the Phantom and I had been dueling for a couple of hours. We both were constantly changing positions, maneuvering about in the palmettos. At the outer edge of the swamp on high ground was a small open pasture—about thirty acres in the shape of a rectangle running long ways by the swamp. The Phantom had somehow managed to make his way to this pasture. He was running from one end of it to another, gobbling, reminding me of Gallberry Joe.

I had hunted this area for some time now. This, coupled with the knowledge I had from my boyhood days, gave me a good idea of the lay of the land. I knew an old long-abandoned public road ran between the swamp and the pasture. It was at one time a stagecoach route running by Lauderdale Springs. These roads are always easy to identify, most of them being very narrow—about eight feet wide. This road had banks about five feet high on each side. I maneuvered around until I got in this old road. I figured it was going to be easy to stay down behind the road bank until I reached the pasture and the Phantom. It worked fine except that bushes were so thick between the road and the pasture it looked like I would not be able to see the Phantom as he paraded along the edge of the pasture.

The road was about forty feet from the pasture's edge and ran parallel to it the entire length. I was slowly moving along the road, careful to stay below the banks. About each ten or fifteen feet, I would ease my head up to try to find an opening through which I could see the pasture. The Phantom was still moving from one end of the pasture to the other. He was passing so close to me, I could hear him walking. I thought if I could find the opening I sought, it would be all over for the Phantom. I had probed the entire distance and was backtracking to look again. Then I found it. It was a small opening and, at places, not more than ten inches in diameter. I raised up to have a good look at the pasture through this small hole and I am sure by now you have guessed that the Phantom was looking through the other end of this tubelike opening. Eyeball to eyeball for a split second. Now you tell me how this durn turkey figured to look at that instant through the only opening there was. Also, how could he see me when I was in deep shadows and he in bright sunlight. Not only did this turkey win this battle, but at that instant, he earned a name: "The Phantom of Possum Creek."

I sat for a few minutes stunned by this sudden change in my duel with the Phantom. The fact that I had lost another battle wasn't the important issue. The issue that was tearing me up was my conscience. Here I was, a supposed-to-be turkey hunter who had stooped so low as to try to bushwhack this turkey. My nefarious scheme had backfired with such a bang that I felt the whole world heard my fall. Now, what all others heard or sensed wasn't important. If, however, the fact became known to Gabe Meadow, it would be at a price I couldn't afford.

I have always made it a practice to investigate all the circumstances related to my losing a battle with a turkey gobbler. What caused it? What change should I have made in tactics? etc. etc. I carefully walked the old road probing for any opening which would permit me to see the pasture. I found the one I looked through to be the only one. Then I went out into the pasture to look over the area from the Phantom's point of view. From that angle I couldn't even find the small opening. Back to the road to put a white handkerchief at the place where my face was when I saw the Phantom. Then to the pasture to bend over at about the same eye level as the turkey and walk slowly looking for the opening so I could see the handkerchief. I never found it.

In turkey hunting you encounter events and happenings that you won't understand. It would be better, I believe, to simply accept it and forget it. I could never do that, and I constantly sought logical answers. I needed logic to keep me from leaning toward the supernatural. I never had this trouble with others in the wildlife community. The deer, fox, coon, wildcat, crow, hawk, and fish never presented anything bordering on the supernatural.

It was spring and the third year to hunt the "Phantom of Possum Creek." This year, like the other two, I eagerly scouted the Possum Creek domain of the Phantom to see if he had survived the long summer and winter following last year's spring turkey season. As stated, there were certain people who would hunt the Phantom year round. I was pleased one morning to make contact with Mr. Phantom. I wasted no time in informing him of my intention of winding up our war. I pointed out to him the fact that I was laying it all on the line: my prestige, my experience, my reputation, my all. I don't believe he was impressed in the least. I was now hunting the Phantom like a hungry panther. We were having some encounters of the fourth, fifth, and sixth kind. Several times I came so close to killing this turkey, only a miracle saved him.

To aid my chances, after every bout with the Phantom I scouted the area to learn more details. One day I discovered a very important fact. I knew the Phantom roosted all over the swamp area. Sometime along its edges, sometime on the west side of Possum Creek, and other times on the east side. I already knew that, regardless of the side he roosted on early in the morning, he would cross the creek to the opposite side. This day I discovered the place where the Phantom usually made his creek crossings. In a heavily wooded area the creek had very high banks, twenty feet or more in height. A huge tree had fallen across the creek at this point. The butt section rested on one bank and the top section with big limbs rested on the other bank. This tree had been a giant in its day, about five feet in diameter. It had been laying across Possum Creek for years, from all appearances. Along the sandy bank of the creek, the Phantom's tracks led to this tree. He was using it as a bridge to cross the creek. His tracks of several ages told that he used his bridge regularly. I sat down to study this development.

I had already committed the sin of trying to ambush this turkey. One more big try should not add much to what I had already done. I decided to build the best blind I knew how on the east bank of Possum Creek, at a point which would be in good gun range of the Phantom as he stepped off his bridge onto the bank. I even found that he had a favorite limb of the tree he would walk out on and, with a little hop, he would be on Possum Creek's east bank. I toted driftwood, logs, and limbs from an area of a hundred yards to my blind site, careful at all times not to use the materials close to the Phantom's bridge. I was proud of my blind. It was well built and comfortable, as I knew it must be. Perhaps it would take days of sitting in it to get a shot at the Phantom. Whatever it took, I was ready to give. After finishing the blind, I walked the log from west to east as it crossed Possum Creek. Every step I carefully studied the blind for some sign of anything which would be a giveaway. I could find none. Now all I needed was to catch the Phantom roosting on the west side of Possum Creek. That chance came quicker than I expected. Three days after building the blind, my owling at daylight brought the Phantom to life with a lusty gobble. He was roosting on the west side of Possum Creek about two hundred fifty yards from the log bridge. I knew the very slough he was roosting over. I had decided not even to yelp but simply to wait him out—an ambush of the lowest kind. I tried to justify it in my mind by reviewing the things the Phantom had done to me. What I really needed was to be more like Gabe in times like this. The more a turkey would outdo Gabe, the more Gabe respected and admired him. It helped a little when I made up my mind one day to sit down and make a complete confession to Gabe all about the Phantom and me.

My blind was constructed so that the hole my gun ran through enabled me to cover the log from bank to bank. I didn't have long to wait. As if by magic, the Phantom appeared at the log on the west side of Possum Creek. What a sight he was. I believe he had the longest legs, body, and neck I ever saw on a wild turkey. Still, he did not appear gaunt but rather lean and graceful. The Phantom went into a half strut, then hopped up on the log to stand tall and survey the scene. His eyes raked everything within a seventy-five-yard circle, including my blind. I was now glad I spent so much time on the blind, as he accepted it. Slowly he strutted along the log until he reached the limb he had been walking out on during his other crossings. At that point, he hesitated and I felt that perhaps I had again been had by Mr. Phantom. I could have killed him at this point, but he would have fallen into the creek. I had already decided to wait until he landed on the bank before I would shoot him. Things started coming my way as he walked out on this huge limb. At about the point where the limb was right over the bank of the creek, the Phantom crouched to hop off on the bank. At that moment the scene exploded. Pandemonium and noise you wouldn't believe. Falling objects and mass confusion. When the crouching Phantom put his weight on the limb, it

The Phantom hopped up on
the log, stood tall, and surveyed
the whole scene.

Success ~ perhaps a hard fought battle with a worthy opponent.

broke with a bang and went crashing into the creek. It scared me so bad, I tore down one side of my blind. From the moment the limb broke, I don't remember seeing the Phantom again. When I regained my senses, I ran to the creek, expecting to see the Phantom in the creek, tangled in the mass of limbs and debris. He wasn't there. I searched the area for hours and probed but no Phantom. This event brought up a host of questions that are hard to answer. I am convinced that this turkey had crossed this log for years. He had also walked out on that particular limb and hopped off it on the bank for years. How was it that it broke at this specific time? What happened to the Phantom when the limb broke? I was within twenty-five steps of him and never saw him after the limb broke.

I never hunted "The Phantom of Possum Creek" again. I found out that he still roamed his palmetto paradise, having survived our last encounter. I believe a little of Gabe's feelings for the wild turkey rubbed off on me at that time. I found myself wanting to remember the Phantom as he was the last day I saw him strutting across Possum Creek on the log.

Now I have two stabilizers: Gabe Meadow and "The Phantom of Possum Creek." Anytime my ego starts to get out of hand, all I have to do is call up one or the other.

8

Kyle Delk

I HAD been hunting turkeys for fifteen or twenty years when I met Kyle Delk for the first time. Gabe Meadow knew Kyle, and I had often heard Gabe mention him. Gabe classed Kyle as one of the best turkey hunters who ever lived. That was enough to make me want to meet and know this man.

Several friends and I were camped on the banks of a river in East Mississippi, setting hooks and trot lines for catfish. The time was midsummer. I had walked a couple of miles to a crossroad store for some supplies. Out front of the store, several men sat talking and I found one was Kyle Delk. I should have known! I have said before there is something about these old master turkey hunters that sets them apart from other men. Kyle wasn't saying a word, just listening, and I knew he wasn't going to stay there long. Kyle lived several miles back in the flatwoods and seldom ventured out of his wooded paradise. When Kyle got up to go, I barged up to him and introduced myself. After giving each other the one pump handshake, Kyle stepped back and looked me over carefully, which, of course, gave me a chance to size him up. Kyle was one of those raw-boned, weatherbeaten men who were ageless. I couldn't begin to guess his age although I knew from what Gabe had said, he must have been older than Gabe, or in his late seventies. He asked me, ''How's your Pa?'' He explained that he knew my people. Later he told me my Daddy had turned a big favor for his family. That explained the fact that he was willing to take up time with me. Fact is, I followed him out to his one-horse wagon and there we had some turkey talk.

Kyle Delk issued me an invitation to come out the next gobbling season and hunt turkeys with him. He agreed to pick me up at this crossroad store the first day of April of next year, explaining that the road to his house at that time of year would be impassable except for horse and wagon. I was to find out in later years that even a four-wheel-drive vehicle would simply not be able to make it on these roads in winter and spring. The roads became ribbons of mud that defied even your walking on it. The mud would build up on your shoe soles until you would have to stop and clean it off. Any wheeled vehicle with fenders over the wheels was doomed. The mud would build up on the tires and finally bind against the fenders and stall the vehicle.

Now, all this was in the best interest of the wild turkey. In fact, I believe it was a big factor in the survival of the wild turkey in this area—that fact and a few men like Kyle Delk who were dedicated to the survival and wellbeing of the wild turkey. The baiting and trapping of wild turkeys was a common practice in most areas and led to the demise of this noble bird. Gabe Meadow had told me how Kyle Delk had almost single handed looked after the wild turkey in an area of ten square miles around his home. "If you mistreated a wild turkey in this flatwood paradise, you would be in trouble with Kyle Delk, and brother, when you were in trouble with Kyle Delk, you were in a heap of trouble," so stated Gabe Meadow.

I have always been fascinated by turkey men like Tony Mc-Cleb, Kyle Delk, and Gabe Meadow and their fight for the survival of the wild turkey. Still, these master turkey hunters would hunt and kill the wild turkey gobbler with such gusto that an observer might believe the hunter was trying to exterminate the wild turkey. Closer observation and you learned that only the gobbler was hunted and killed. Further you learned that the gobbler was hunted only during the spring gobbling season. Every master turkey huntter I ever knew had one thing in common. They would kill only mature turkey gobblers and only at spring gobbling time.

Most people know that the true character of a person is what

The wild turkey's reflexes are good enough to pick flying insects out of the air with ease.

As Kyle plowed his patches
this old character turkey
would frequently be in the
same patch.

a person does and thinks when he knows his acts and thoughts will not be revealed to others. So it is with a master turkey hunter as his status as a turkey hunter develops. His actions toward the wild turkey, and even his thoughts, must be within the unwritten, but understood, laws and rules of the dedicated turkey hunter.

Kyle told me of this character turkey and the many battles with him. How this turkey would know when the season of hunting was over and the summer, autumn, and winter truce would be on. Now, mind you, this was Kyle's own arrangement, because at that time Kyle had never heard of gamewardens, open and closed seasons, or game and bag limits. Kyle would be trying to plant his little corn patches and this durn character turkey would be brazen enough to follow him up and down the rows, picking up the seed corn he had dropped. Sometime the turkey would even scratch up corn which had come up to get at the kernel at the roots. Kyle said as he plowed his patches, this old character would frequently be in the same patch with him and, at times, so close it would have been easy to kill him. Every now and then, as the turkey would be real brazen and brave, Kyle would shout at him, "You devil, git from here." Kyle would then stop his horse and run at the turkey whereupon the turkey would amble off a little ways, turn and gobble at Kyle. Now, it never occurred to Kyle to kill this turkey during the "truce," even though the turkey harassed Kyle no end. Kyle wanted this turkey to survive to do battle with him during spring gobbling time. Kyle said he would be planning some special tricks to pull on this particular turkey.

Back in the old days when turkey hunters got together for turkey talk, the talk wasn't about how many did you kill. Rather, each hunter would inquire of the others, "Have you run into any characters lately?" If, in fact, a hunter had run into a character turkey, this hunter would have the attention of all the other hunters. It is a natural thing for a good turkey hunter to want to hear of the tricks and tactics of a wild turkey who is able to outdo the hunter.

I wanted to find out from Kyle Delk about the character turkeys he had hunted. Of course, Kyle had over the years run into several and each one stood out vividly in Kyle's mind. Matter of fact, the turkey that followed Kyle in his fields was a real character. He said this turkey had already whipped him two seasons. "One year," said Kyle, "I had hunted this durn turkey like a hungry panther. He was proving to be my match. Every trick I knew, I pulled on him, and he took them in stride. I came mighty close to bagging him on several occasions. Once it seemed like I was sure to kill him. He was walking this path straight to me and was getting in range, when he suddenly whirled and flew. I was puzzled because I knew he hadn't seen me. I walked out to the path where he took off from to look. There laying in the middle of the path was my corn cob pipe which I had lost more than a week ago. I have heard that turkeys can't smell very well. Mindy said if that old pipe had been laying there a week, the smell coming from it would be so thick it could be seen. Now that's kind of jokey but it is a fact that this smart devil spooked at my pipe." Kyle was enjoying telling about this character turkey and I was, of course, eating it up.

"Another time," continued Kyle, "I cam mighty close to bagging Corn." Corn was the simple name Kyle had given this character turkey. Kyle said it helped him remember how this turkey bugged him during corn planting time. Kyle said, "As you now know, I like to have open woods when I sit to a turkey. Just a good big tree to sit in front of. I've had very little trouble with turkeys seeing me. Knowing, however, that Corn was not a ordinary run-of-the-mill wild turkey, I decided to cut me a nice little cedar tree about four feet high to stick up in front. I toted this durn tree around that spring till I near wore it out. Stuck it up in front of me lots of times. Killed several turkeys with it stuck up, but not Corn. One day, I was working Corn with my little tree stuck up in front. For some unexplained reason, Corn was coming to me straight as a martin to his gourd. I had laid back the hammers on ole Betsy and they looked like the ears of a rabbit laying in his bed. Trusty ole double-barreled Betsy was ready. Corn was now in range, walking slowly, head held high. What a turkey he was. I was as taut as a fiddle string. I was getting ready to squeeze the

It is a fact that this smart devil spooked at my pipe.

Night hunter

trigger when something fell on me. It near scared the daylights out of me and Corn too. The durn little tree had keeled over and fell in my lap at the time I was so worked up at the sight of Corn. How it fell, I don't know, but somehow strange things just seem to come along when you get tangled with a character turkey."

Kyle and Mindy Delk lived in a small house. It was in the middle of some of the finest timberland in the south—an area called "flatwoods" by the natives. The land had a very gentle roll—no hills and no levels. When I hunted for the first time in this area, I found out how easy it was to get lost, especially on a cloudy day. Now, you could usually work your way out but likely you would be several miles from your goal when you finally came to a place familiar to you.

I believe Kyle owned about one-hundred twenty acres but he benefited from several thousand acres. His nearest neighbor was five miles away. Kyle had about twenty small patches which he cultivated. He planted five each year and let the other fifteen lay out and rest. Each patch of about an acre thus regained natural fertility. Now these patches that were not being cultivated were natural nesting sites for turkey, quail, and all kinds of other birds and animals. For years and years, Kyle and his ancestors had planted and protected every kind of nut and berry in an area surrounding the cultivated patches. Not only did this suffice to feed the Delks, but the surplus attracted the wildlife of the area in unbelievable numbers.

For many years, the natives who lived around the outer boundaries of "the flatwoods" would release hogs, who thrived wild and unattended in this wooded paradise. Cattle, too, were allowed to roam free range in the area.

I often have thought how easy it was for the Delks to live in this unspoiled, wild, and beautiful land. I came to know these people very well. I tried to help with the chores to kind of earn my keep. The Delks knowledge of preserving the bounty of their fields and woods was astounding. Their knowledge of the wildlife at their doorsteps was incredible.

One morning Kyle and I were coming back from planting a patch of corn. Close to the trail which led to the house, Kyle spotted the remains of a turkey gobbler. Kyle picked up the carcass and examined it carefully. He then rendered his verdict of the cause of this killing—owl. I really had never thought of an owl as an enemy of an adult wild turkey. Kyle said the big horned owl could easily kill a big turkey gobbler. The owl, a natural night hunter, would find a turkey roosting on a branch of a tree. The owl would get between the turkey and the trunk of the tree and start pushing the turkey toward the end of the limb. After a while, the turkey would be pushed off the end of the limb and the owl would grab the turkey and litterally ride him to the ground. The poor turkey, of course, couldn't see and the owl could and that fact spelled the outcome of the battle. Kyle said he didn't believe an owl would tackle an adult turkey in daylight.

Kyle had one small garden which had a picket or rived paling fence around it. The pickets were close enough to keep out rabbits. Kyle said one spring a tame turkey hen flew over this fence and established a nest in the corner of the garden. She had laid and was setting on twelve eggs in the nest when this big chicken snake crawled through the fence and swallowed every egg in the nest. With all these eggs inside him, the snake was unable to squeeze back through the fence to freedom. After a while, Mindy discovered the snake and Kyle killed Mr. Snake without breaking a single egg. The eggs were taken out of the snake and returned to the nest. Every egg hatched and Kyle said raised without their knowing about their Jonah act— being in the belly of a reptile.

I visited the Delks at different times of the year and always tried to bring them some small token to show my appreciation of their hospitality: a pair of scissors for Mindy, a good pocket knife for Kyle. I purposely kept the gifts small to keep them from feeling that I was trying to pay for my keep. With these fiercely independent, wonderful people, anything looking like a bribe or payment for hospitality would have injured their pride beyond repair. I needed them a lot more than they needed me. How many people in this world get an opportunity to see another world? How many get to actually be a part of it for even a short time?

This crisp spring morning, Kyle and I were heading for the old Stanton field to listen for a gobbler. I followed closely behind Kyle as he trod the dim trail this pre-dawn morning. I was having trouble keeping up, as this agile old man seemed to glide along silently and effortlessly. The old Stanton field contained about forty acres, and its relatively flat top rose up out of the flat woods to form a hammock. At one time, an ancient family of pioneers lived here and cultivated this field. Wild turkeys were particularly fond of this old field for nesting. Kyle said in spring you could always find some good gobblers around this old field, because lots of hens would be present. How right he was.

As day started breaking, Kyle and I were standing in the middle of Stanton field. Kyle said, "Do some owling." I didn't get to owl much because several real owls answered me and set up a continual chatter among themselves. All this owl talk brought on the turkey talk. Now, I have heard a lot of turkeys gobble during my half-century of exposure to them, but the gobbling I heard that morning long ago beats anything I have ever heard. This brings up a point I have been thinking on long and serious. Is the gobbling of the wild turkey going to fade away? Will it be that eventually a turkey hunter will hunt turkeys and never hear the war cry of the turkey gobbler? Without exception every old master turkey hunter would tell about the tremendous amount of gobbling wild turkey did years ago. Audubon spoke of it. Gradually, down through the years, wild turkeys in our part of the country are gobbling less and less. This, I believe, is due to the tremendous amount of pressure from hunters put on the gobbling turkey. At the same time, the gobbler who won't gobble has the best chance to survive. The loud mouth gobbling turkey is thus replaced by the silent one who lives to breed and pass on his genes. I read of areas where newly stocked wild turkeys protected from hunting pressures gobble like in the old days in our part of the country. Everyone who hunts turkeys knows how difficult it is to kill a mature wild gobbler who won't gobble.

The gobbling around Stanton Field that morning was being done by what Kyle and I guessed would be fifteen mature gobblers. The air was cool and crisp and I believe we were hearing turkeys in an area of about fifteen hundred acres. Kyle would turn his head as each new gobbler opened up. After a few minutes Kyle said, "Pick one that you want to work with and I'll go to one in the opposite direction."

The turkey I chose had the shrill voice and rattle of a mature turkey. I had suspected that most any gobbler in this area would have hens with him. I also knew these hens would be roosting in kind of a cluster; and the gobbler, a hundred yards or so off to himself. Exactly so. I was able to get in good position to my gobbler and he answered my yelps with enthusiasm. However, before he was half way to me, hens began to surround him and my chance faded. My spirit further took a nose dive when I heard Kyle's old double-barrel boom away. When I got up with Kyle, he had a fine old turkey slung across his shoulder. Kyle carried a rawhide thong about thirty inches long with a loop in each end. One loop over the dead turkey's head and the other loop over the feet and the center of the thong over the shoulder so you could carry a turkey real easy. Always the head of the turkey should be in front when carrying.

Kyle wanted me to tell him about my turkey and I laid out the story simple and true. True friend, good old unselfish Kyle at that point gave me some of the best advice I ever had. Kyle drew it out slowly as if wanting to let it soak in good. "You know most old gobblers are going to have his harem of hens with him this time of year. They shield his old ornery hide from danger. He lets them walk ahead and take all the risks. Still, he won't roost with them at night. He is going to be stuck off to himself and come morning is going to let the hens fly down first. If any danger is present, he'll get up with them and begin showing off for their benefit. Now, for you to deal with this gobbler with his hens, this is what you do. First, you locate the gobbler and slip up within about one to two hundred yards of him. You know that the hens are near, so you start some low tree yelps to locate the hens. Another good way to start hens yelping is to make a continual low, clicking noise with your tongue. Slowly and quietly you move in a circle, keeping about the same distance from the gobbler until you locate the hens. This whole operation must be done after the first light of day and before normal fly-down time. The hens most likely will be roosting close together but each may be in a different tree. You ease around and get between the gobbler and these hens. Start flushing the hens away from the gobbler and try to flush them one at a time. What you are doing is making the gobbler believe the hens are just flying down normal-like. When you do all this proper, the gobbler has been put on an equal with you because it's one-on-one again. Fact is, the odds have turned in your favor because of these hens. He knows they are out there because he heard them fly down.''

I guess one day I would have worked out this tactic for myself as it seemed so simple and logical. Still, I know many turkey hunters who have been hunting for years and couldn't cope with this situation. Many is the time you will hear a turkey hunter say, "I had him coming to me, strutting and gobbling, until these hens got up with him and that ended my chance for the day.''

While we are on the subject of turkey hens and the hazard they present to the turkey hunter, let me give some advice of my own. I kind of worked this out on my own and it has sure worked for me. Let's say you are working a gobbler and a hen or group of hens come along and take him away from you. Most people would simply give up. You don't have to. After the gobbler and hens have been together for a while, they will begin to move slowly on a distinct course. This course could carry them along an old road, along a ridge, or along a valley. As they travel, the hens will always be in front with the gobbler trailing. Every now and then the gobbler will catch up with the hens and strut around, showing off. Your job is to find out the direction they are going and to stay within yelping distance. If the gobbler will answer each time you yelp, it makes your task much easier to keep contact without being seen. If the gobbler won't answer your yelping, your job is harder but not impossible. Simply stay far enough behind so as not to be seen. This will test your woodsmanship and patience. As you follow these turkeys, yelping at intervals, there is a good chance the gobbler will come to you. He doesn't like to have a hen tagging behind. He wants her up front. Each time you stop to yelp be sure you are prepared for the gobbler if he decides at that point to drop back and pick up this trailing hen. I have killed many fine old gobblers with this tactic and it is well within Gabe's rules of proper methods. Fact is, Gabes rules don't tend to inhibit a turkey hunter; they tend to make his hunting more enjoyable because you have had to work at it.

Kyle Delk, like most people I have known who lived close to nature, had a great sense of humor. One day we were sitting on the bank of a creek. At this point, the banks were high and a log lay across the creek from bank to bank. A natural foot log for man and wild creatures wanting to cross the creek. About middle way of the log, several limbs stuck out. A gray squirrel hopped up on this log and he had in his mouth a huge deer antler. When the squirrel reached the point on the log where the limbs were, he couldn't get through on account of the width of the antlers. Several times the squirrel tried to go through to no avail. Kyle and I were watching with interest. At one point, the squirrel came back to the end of the log, laid the antlers down and went back out to see if he could walk the length of the log. Of course he could, and he seemed to ponder the situation. Finally after much thought, trials, and failures, the squirrel brought the antlers back to the end of the log and vigorously began to eat them. Kyle said, "Now there is a smart squirrel. He has finally figured out how to get them through the limbs: in his belly."

In my mind, Kyle and Mindy Delk qualified as true pioneers. The fact that this ingenious couple could live so close to nature and partake of its bounty without spoiling even one phase of nature's plan made them great, to my way of thinking.

One thing nearly all old master turkey hunters had in common was their want to share with you some of the old and corny "turkey tales" of years ago. I found out early that this was a price you simply must pay if you were to gain and retain favor with them. It is quite possible some of these old "turkey tales" had as their basis some true facts. All of them were handed down generation to generation by word of mouth and that, no doubt, would tend to make them unbelievable.

After the squirrel and horn episode, Kyle took the light mood of both of us to tell me about "the turkey, the farmer, and the blackberry patch." I had already heard this tale several times, but didn't let that fact be known. Poor old Kyle was not in the class with Tony McCleb and some other yarn spinners I knew but then he simply did not have the audiences they had had.

Kyle said this farmer was busy plowing his fields when he noticed this wild turkey gobbler go up a hill at the same time each day. When the farmer checked into this, he found the turkey was going up the hill to a blackberry patch. A sandy path wound its way from the bottom to the top of the hill. Not being a turkey hunter, the farmer decided to go up the hill to the blackberry patch at the proper time and ambush this turkey. The farmer went up to the top of the hill, hid himself, and waited and waited. No turkey. Several days the farmer would go up and wait. Still no turkey. When the farmer would go back to his plowing, he would see the turkey go up the hill each day. Now this farmer had heard the tales told by turkey hunters. How a wild turkey could outmaneuver a man was legendary. The farmer was being taught a lesson. The more the turkey eluded him, the more time he spent trying to bag the turkey, and the grassier his fields became. For five days straight, the farmer sat by the blackberry patch. But no turkey. On the fifth day, as the farmer came back down the hill from his vigil, he caught a glimpse of the turkey approaching the path at the foot of the hill. The turkey miraculously did not see the farmer, who hid quickly at the edge of the path. The turkey nonchalantly walked up to the path and saw the fresh tracks of the farmer going up the hill and back down the hill. Without hesitation, the turkey then went up the hill to his blackberry patch. The farmer could hardly believe his eyes. If a turkey hunter had told him this story, the farmer would have branded him as an outright liar. The farmer plowed his fields and pondered the situation. One day an idea struck the farmer. The next morning the farmer strapped his gun on his back and headed for the path. On his feet he wore his shoes as usual. On his hands he put another pair of shoes with the toes backwards. The farmer then carefully walked up the path to the blackberry patch on his all fours, making two sets of tracks. One set of tracks going up the hill, the other set seeming to come down the hill. The farmer didn't have long to wait. Along comes Mr. Turkey and examines the tracks and calmly walks up the hill toward the blackberry patch. Mr. Gobbler never reached the blackberry patch, as the farmer bushwhacked him forthwith, and the blackberries ripened in the warm sun.

Kyle and I were in the old Stanton Field one day when he told me about the last of the Stantons who lived there. Kyle said Lane Stanton was a bachelor and the last person to live in the old Stanton house. Lane was a loner and the place he lived was sure suited to him. Kyle said when he was a boy he used to go over to see Mr. Lane Stanton. One day he was at Mr. Stanton's house and it was time to start cooking supper. Mr. Stanton told Kyle to go to the kitchen with him and this was the first time Kyle had seen this room. Kyle had heard rumors about some of Mr. Stanton's peculiar ways. In the country in those days, starting a fire was an art. Mr. Stanton was going to start one now in the stove. Along the entire wall on one side of the kitchen were twenty to thirty small boxes about a foot square. Each had a lid hinged with a piece of leather. Mr. Stanton walked over to these boxes, raised a couple of lids and got enough dry straw and twigs to start his fire. Kyle said he was amazed. Mr. Stanton told him to go outside and see that there was a small hole leading to each box on the inside. Mr. Stanton said the birds worked hard building nests in the boxes, which keep him in tinder for his fires.

Kyle and I hunted together for many years, this man being one of the most remarkable people I have ever known. He told me about many of his experiences with and his love for the wild turkey, above all other creatures.

Kyle said every now and then some new people would take up turkey hunting. Some new hunters would, on occasion, get as far back in the woods as Kyle's domain. Most of these people would be hunters and woodsmen but not trained in the art of turkey hunting. Some of them would be expert deer hunters, squirrel hunters, quail hunters, etc., and they would be too proud to ask advice of a turkey hunter. Instead, they would strike out on their own, determined to prove that a good hunter of other game could also bag a wild turkey. After a few hunts and some unbelievable events, they would be ashamed to admit what was taking place. It is hard to believe to what ends some of these people would go to try to overcome their failure.

For miles in every direction around Kyle's home, the country was free range. In other words, branded cattle were allowed to roam free throughout the whole area. A lot of farmers would put cow bells on some of their cows, which would help them locate the cows. Some said each bell would have its own distinct sound and the farmer could locate his cows by it. In winter and early spring, some farmers would take ear corn out to the area that they found their cows to be using. This corn would be scattered about and the cows would soon discover it and it would help them at that time of year. When the cows would eat this corn, some grains would pass through the cow's digestive system and come out whole and be in the cow's dung or droppings. The turkeys would soon discover that cows were dropping corn and it would be amusing to Kyle to see turkeys following these belled cows.

Kyle said one day he heard this bell tingling as a cow approached his position. Kyle stepped back off the trail to observe the oncoming cow and perhaps the turkeys who might be following. To Kyle's utter amazement what he saw coming down the path was not a cow at all but a man with a cow hide draped over his body and a cow bell around his neck. Even had a set of horns, and it all looked real. Kyle watched this apparition pass but no turkeys were following. Kyle was so fascinated, he decided to follow and perhaps learn who was under the cow hide. The man was doing a good job, swinging along and causing the bell to ring. Every now and then, he would stop and turn around in hopes that a turkey would be following. It was no trouble for woodwise Kyle to follow and stay out of sight. The hide-covered man seemed to be having difficulty at times seeing well enough to travel over rough places. He was frequently stumbling, and at one real rough place, he suddenly fell sprawling.

When he had laid there for a minute or more, Kyle became concerned and quickly went up to him to render aid. Kyle admitted to me that his curiosity was aroused to find out who was under the hide. When he helped the man to his feet, he did so in such a way that the cowhide slipped away to reveal old Doctor Sam Smythe. Now, if Kyle had been trying to guess who was under the hide, Doctor Sam would be the last guess. Doctor Sam was a dignified country doctor whom Kyle had never seen without a stiff high collar and black string tie. Doctor Sam was a very popular man and was the one who kept the whole community buzzing with fun and laughter. His banter of the hunters and fishermen was legendary and his sharp wit kept them constantly on guard to keep Doc from finding out about some of their exploits. Now Kyle and Doctor Sam were eye ball to eye ball and in a situation where Kyle held the unbelievable position of top hand. Kyle was such a man that he did not tell me what really took place on that eventful day. He didn't tell me what overtures the poor old Doc made toward him in order to keep this thing quiet. Actually no one Kyle knew had ever heard of the doctor hunting or fishing. Kyle said for me to keep this to myself. I knew the doctor must have come up with some form of bribe—perhaps free medical care. Maybe this was the beginning of medicare.

Kyle really got a kick out of Doc and his exploit. It was hard for Kyle to believe and, had he not seen with his own eyes, would not accept it as the truth. To me, there was a logical answer and this was not the first time these things ran through my mind. I believe there is an inborn instinct in every human being on this earth to hunt. We all hunt. The baby hunts something to meddle. The boy hunts his lost knife. The young man hunts a wife. The wife hunts food to prepare for her family. The inventor hunts new and useful objects. For millions and millions of years, man hunted to survive. A great thrill came to man when suddenly, food for the family would appear in the form of a pig, a deer, or a turkey. When a wild turkey gobbles at you today, that tingle along your spine and the nape of your neck is part of your instinct rising up. Man is not alone in having his instincts revert to the past. Observe old Fluffy, the Persian cat who is the family pet. Docile and tame, old Fluffy likes to be held and petted. But let old Fluffy wander into a wooded area and suddenly this cat creature is a hunter and a super stalker and his love for it shows in every movement of his body. Only during the last few thousand years has man been able to survive without his individual efforts as a hunter. Three to five hundred times that long he had to hunt to survive, and that much time builds instincts.

This is what I believe happened in Doc's case. The old Doc, being a very intelligent man, had heard the many tales told by turkey hunters. He had probably been paid his fee in the form of a wild turkey on occasions. The Doc had probably been carrying his shotgun with him as he made his rounds with horse and buggy. When early in the morning an old gobbler would sound off close to the road, old Doc would hitch his horse and ease out for a try at Mr. Turkey. The Doc figured if he could bag a gobbler, he could have a lot of fun with the turkey hunters, rubbing it in on them. I have known lots of people who took up turkey hunting for this very same reason. Now in Doc's case, a natural progression set in. Doc actually began to enjoy these little forays as his instincts took over. As usual in these instances, the turkey always won.

Doc had observed the turkeys following the cows and, being of inventive mind, figured out the cowhide bell-ringing technique. I guess lots of folks would consider old Doc slipping around in the woods draped in a cowhide with a cow bell around his neck a very unprofessional act. I don't. This is what wild turkeys do to people. Stranger things than this have taken place during man's confrontations with turkeys. As in the case of Doc, it is by sheer accident that some of these strange events come to light. For the benefit of the younger generation, doctors used to make house calls. The old doctor with his lightweight buggy, good horse, and black bag is a part of our heritage. I have thought how tough it would be to be in severe pain and waiting for the doctor and said doctor would be in the woods having the daylight whipped out of him by an old turkey gobbler. Even today, doctors seem to have a great desire to turkey hunt. I'm not wanting to infer, however, that ever time your doctor gets "out of pocket" he's turkey hunting. Still it could very well be so.

Now that I had hunted and associated with Kyle Delk, it brought to three the great master turkey hunters I knew so well. At times I would be tempted to try to rate the three: Kyle Delk, Gabe Meadow, and Tony McCleb. In my mind I would pit one against the other in kind of a hunt off. Then I would quit comparing them because if I really found out their rank, it would make me sad. There just didn't seem to be a second or third place for any of them. If, however, some day the great scorer does elect to rank all the master turkey hunters of all time, I believe these great men would rank one, two, three. In which order, I don't want to know.

9

My First Thirty-Three Years

REMEMBERING dates is not one of my best talents. I do, however, remember the spring of 1925 when I bagged my first wild turkey gobbler. For fifty-two consecutive years since that date, I have hunted and killed wild turkeys.

Looking back over the fifty-three years, I find a vast difference in turkey hunting, old style and new style. In deciding at what point the great change came, I have concluded it occurred about twenty years ago. So, I am going to divide my whole career into two parts: *My First Thirty-Three Years* and *My Last Twenty Years.*

Most of this book, up to this point, covers my first thirty-three years. The era of Gabe Meadow, Kyle Delk, and Tony McCleb. The era of classical woods-hunting of gobbling turkeys in the springtime. Without a doubt this is the most challenging way to hunt turkeys. Gabe Meadow would say, "You go into the woods with gun and call—that's all." During this era a hunter had to work hard to get results. The turkey population was much smaller and hunting pressure on the available huntable turkey supply was great. Unless a novice hunter had a good turkey hunter to help him, the learning process was painfully slow and frustrating. Now we have fine vehicles which literally carry us to the roost tree, camouflage clothes which aid us in sitting concealed as our turkey approaches, insecticides which keep the worrisome insects at bay, better turkey calls, magnum guns and magnum ammo which greatly increase the killing range. These vast improvements, of course, apply to the classical woods-hunting of turkeys. We are not, at this point, even going into the more recent methods of hunting which will be explained in the next chapter, "My Last Twenty Years."

I was a member of a hunting club in south Mississippi. The club was primarily a deer club but the area had a good turkey population. I was the only turkey hunter in the bunch. Every spring, however, these deer hunters would come in droves to the club to try their hand at turkey hunting. These hunters were a fine likable bunch of men and most were expert deer hunters. They were loud and boisterous, which seems to be an asset to deer hunters. They never understood why the same slam-banging, wild, and woolly approach failed to produce turkeys.

Early in the spring season one year, twelve of these deer hunters were at the clubhouse to turkey hunt. In the group were two brothers who were civil engineers by profession. One of the engineer brothers was sitting at the edge of a small clearing in the woods late one afternoon. A big turkey gobbler came along and flew up to roost just out of gun range. The engineer sat silently until black dark before slipping away from the roosting turkey. When this man reached camp, he reported the happening to his brother. The two brothers then began to plan strategy. After much discussion and haggling, they decided to let the other deer hunters in on the bagging of this gobbler. In the meantime, I was trying to get a little sleep and rest. When they took in the balance of the bunch of deer hunters, it brought on a deluge of loud and long vocal planning. I lay in my bunk, amused at first, and as the night wore on, my amusement turned to some scheme to quiet this bunch. I had heard my name mentioned several times, followed usually by roars of laughter. The gist of this was how Gene Nunnery was going to react when they hauled in this big gobbler. Seeing as how sleeping was out of the question, I got up and joined them. The engineer brothers had mapped a plan whereby the turkey was bound to be killed by some member of the party. With the tools of their trade, a huge map was drawn on the tablecloth. "X" marked the tree with the roosting gobbler in its branches. Each of the twelve hunters was assigned a position a certain distance from the turkey. When all men were in position, the turkey would be completely surrounded. Then, too, the men would be close enough to each other so that no way could the gobbler get out of the circle without being within range of a man. Dire threats were made on the life of the man who would miss this turkey when he passed by him. These men had even decided to have a big dinner, and all their wives and children would help eat Mr. Gobbler.

I said to the bunch, "Men, if you will be quiet for a minute, I have a proposition for you. The fact is, that you are going to take unfair advantage of that poor gobbler. Consider the odds— twelve of you against one turkey. You know exactly where he is and he doesn't even know you are in this county. But in spite of all that, here is what I am willing to do. I am going to put $5.00 in this jar for each of you. That's sixty dollars. If you bring in that gobbler, you pick up the money and hunt as long as you like after that. But, if you don't have that gobbler here at the camphouse by 9:00 o'clock in the morning, you lose the money. In addition, you agree if you don't kill the turkey, to pack up your gear and go home and allow me to turkey hunt in peace." Man, that brought on long and loud howls of disagreement as to what they should do. Mind you, all this at one o'clock in the morning. Finally when they kind of settled down, I suggested they take a vote on the proposition. The vote was seven to five in favor of accepting my challenge.

I didn't even hunt that morning. I took a chair and sat in the camphouse yard as the twelve departed. The tree the turkey was roosting in was well within range of hearing a gunshot from my position. Time rolled by and as the nine o'clock deadline approached, the haggard bunch began to drift into camp. I had heard no shots and, as I anticipated, this old gobbler had whipped the whole bunch.

After all the hunters had arrived at camp, worn and downhearted, I asked them to explain why their plan didn't work. At first they didn't want to talk about it. Finally one of the engineer brothers volunteered to tell me. He said all twelve men carried out their assignment to the letter. When he heard the old gobbler start gobbling at first light, he knew all the men

were in position and it would simply be a matter of time before someone would make the kill. He said the gobbler must
have gobbled fifteen times in the tree. "I could almost see the
tree he was in and I watched the area carefully," stated John
the engineer. John then asked me sheepishly, "Do you know
what that durn gobbler did?" I shook my head and John continued, "That devil rocketed out of that tree straight up. At
about seventy-five or eighty yards above the tree tops, he set his
wings and sailed right over Earl Dowd, clucking up a storm.
By the time Earl could get his gun up, the durn turkey must
have been crossing over Highway 17, heading west. Earl said
the turkey must have been one hundred yards high and even if
he had been expecting him, the turkey was far out of range."

The deer hunters began to pack their gear to go home to ful-
fill that part of our bargain. I kind of felt sorry for them and
said, "You boys don't have to leave, I will cancel that part of
our agreement." To a man they agreed it would best that they
go home. "No way," they said, "are we going to stay here
with a turkey hunter and have to put up with the static this
episode is going to bring on." At that, this may have been a
wise decision on their part.

I guess it's natural for a man who hunts turkeys for many
years to develop idiosyncrasies. He spends long hours by himself and in an environment that lends itself to having fixed ideas
on most any subject. Gabe told me about this old turkey hunter
who told him it was bad luck to have women folks handle your
clothes during turkey season. This old man by the name of Jody
Jason had lots of fixed ideas about turkeys and turkey hunters.
Gabe said you could always learn something from another turkey
hunter. I agree with that completely. I have found that even a
novice hunter will at times come up with a good tactic or idea.
For this reason, most old turkey hunters will listen attentively as
a young hunter tells about his battle with a turkey gobbler.

Gabe said Jody told him, "Never wash your turkey hunting
clothes. The more they are worn, the softer and more mottled
they become. If they get smelly, just hang them on a fence and
let the sun and wind wash them." Jody then told Gabe about
being in South Alabama hunting turkeys. He went by a friend's

house to go into town with him. Jody had brought a change of clothes and he switched at the friend's house. He left his hunting clothes in the guest room. Late that afternoon, Jody and his friend came home to find that his friend's wife had washed, starched, and ironed the old man's hunting clothes. Jody said it took him the balance of that season and nigh to the middle of the next season to "break in" his clothes again.

I am not quite as set in my ways as Jody Jason, but I discovered early in my career the advantage of having a place set aside for all my turkey hunting gear. Each spring I clean out a space in my den. Every article I use during the whole season is put in this space. Gun, ammo, clothes, boots, insecticides, compass, turkey calls, and twice that many other items I will need. As my children came along, each had to be taught not to touch a single thing in that big pile of "turkey gear." When you get up at three o'clock in the morning, it sure helps to know where everything is. All this arrangement won't come easy. First you have to convince the wife you mean business.

I would be remiss at this point if I failed to bring up a very important issue. Any person who becomes a confirmed turkey hunter must have the cooperation of those around him: his employer or employees, his friends, his kinfolk, and, most important of all, his immediate family. I have trained a few young turkey hunters. An important part of the training is to advise these young hunters how to deal with the little woman. Don't just up and announce that a complete change of living habits is about to take place. To avoid a revolution, you resort to evolution. Work out a system of very slowly gaining a point or two each year. After about ten years, you should have your family willing to accept the fact that you are going to turkey hunt every morning of open turkey season. Additionally, there may be a week or so of scouting before the season opens. It is a known and accepted fact that the first light of day is the prime time to turkey hunt. That being so, means the turkey hunter must get out of bed an hour or two before daybreak. If you must get up at three o'clock in the morning, go to bed by nine o'clock at the latest. For many years I have started my early-to-bed, early-to-rise routine a week or so before the season begins. That way you get used to it and feel good early in the morning. You need to be in top form, mentally and physically, to cope with a wild turkey. I completely agree with the statement Gabe Meadow once made. Gabe said, "To become a real successful turkey hunter, a man has to have a wife who completely approves of his hunting. If she disapproves, forget about turkeys."

The two main things a turkey gobbler does that fascinates a hunter is his gobbling and his strutting. Normally he does a lot of both. A turkey's gobbling and strutting are his trademark. I don't recall reading even one of the many good turkey stories that doesn't stress the gobbling of the turkey. I admit, the telling of the way the gobbler responded to the hunter's calls by gobbling is colorful. A big gobbler in full strut is about the prettiest sight a hunter's eye can see. I have no argument with outdoor writers who color their stories about wild turkeys with gobbling and strutting. Also, turkey hunters themselves, in giving their account of a battle with a turkey gobbler, spice it with the strutting and gobbling of their adversary. This brings me to the point I want to make—the fact that a novice turkey hunter has both heard and read what a turkey gobbler does when you call to him. This novice hunter, from the evidence presented him, believes every wild turkey gobbler is going to strut and gobble. Most do, but what about the ones who don't answer you with a gobble?

If you have just started turkey hunting, I want you to carefully read and reread the following lines about a wild turkey's reactions when you call to him. Take my word for it, the situation I now describe will happen to you many times when you hunt the wild turkey. Say you have located a turkey gobbler. Perhaps you saw or heard him as he flew up to roost. Or you may have started him gobbling at the first light of day. Anyway, this early morning you have moved close enough to this turkey gobbler to call to him. You have selected the place you will sit. The showdown is coming rapidly. The next fifteen minutes or so are going to be the most important time of your hunt. From your position, you make your call to the gobbler and he doesn't make a sound. You know he has heard you and you don't understand why he didn't answer you with a gobble like the book says. The fact that this turkey didn't answer you could be the sign that you have a smart old trophy gobbler on your hands. If, in fact, you have this wise old gobbler on your hands, he is not going to sit and gobble or come strutting to you. Likely he is going to spread his wings and float down from his roost like a dry autumn leaf on a frosty morning. Hardly a thud will be heard as his feet hit the ground. Once he is on the ground, he begins to stalk you—you become the hunted. He knows exactly where you are but you don't know where he is; like a light puff of smoke, he is going to drift through the forest silently and slowly. He tacks and circles to observe your position from many angles. He stops frequently and may stand behind a tree or a bush for extended periods of time. Since leaving his roost tree, this turkey has not strutted or gobbled. He walks upright with his head held unbelievably high. As he slowly moves along, his head is constantly turning and his fantastic eyes see everything in his range of vision. He is looking for movement. No movement escapes his keen eyes. If this turkey is moving around in cover, chances are you have not seen him. If you have moved during all this time, he has seen you and has melted into the woods and as Tobe Sill said, "evaporated before your eyes."

As I said in the beginning of this advice on dealing with a silent old gobbler, very few gobblers act this way. I have found that the few who do refuse to answer a call will be among the best turkeys you will kill. To me that's what it's all about: finding a wise old gobbler who will test your skill as a turkey hunter.

So now you know what could be taking place when you call to a gobbler and he gives you the silent treatment. If you have heeded the advice of Gabe Meadow and learned to sit to a turkey, your chances to kill this old trophy turkey are good. Most turkeys answer you with a gobble; a few don't and I thought you ought to know.

You will note that I have not dwelled on the type of calls you want to make to attract your gobbler. There is a very distinct and divided school of thought on this subject. I believe the hunters who advocate very little yelping and very soft are mostly older hunters. The younger people who hunt turkeys seem to want to keep up a constant chatter in talking to a gobbler. Why should I attempt to make the decision as to which is best. I will leave it up to the wild turkey gobblers to decide which he likes best. I do know there are many fine turkey hunters who like to yelp softly and very little. On the other hand, a large group of people yelp and cluck and gobble loud and long and have good results. The mating call of the wild turkey hen is three to five rapid yelps done very softly. Most all turkey hunters agree on that. Most all hunters also agree the mating call is the most effective call you can use and perhaps the most widely used. The cackle and yelp of the turkey hen is a fine call. Many good turkey hunters use it. Some hunters use only the cluck and that, too, is effective. The hunters who gobble to a wild gobbler swear by that call. Try several calls to find the one that works best for you. Then stick with the chosen one. You know by now, as this book has taught, some turkey gobblers simply won't come to a turkey call. On certain days and with some turkeys, a turkey hunter must have a bag of tricks available at all times. If you have carefully read this book, you should have picked up many ideas and maneuvers effective in dealing with a stubborn gobbler. I know some nefarious ways to take a gobbler. I have never used them and will not reveal them for fear some desperate hunter may resort to their use.

You have learned from the pages of this book that it is no disgrace to be bested by a turkey gobbler. When you hunt by Gabe's rules, losing a battle to a turkey gobbler is surely going to happen. If you can't accept this defeat at the feet of a turkey gobbler, you should give up turkey hunting. Take my word for it, some of the richest treasures in your memory bank will be the times an old turkey gobbler "put it on you." Perhaps you don't want to just take my word for this. In that case I call up Gabe Meadow, Tony McCleb, and Kyle Delk, who, without exception, would vouch for this. Every now and then, as you meet and talk to turkey hunters, you will run into a person who will make this claim. "I can call up and kill any turkey gobbler that walks." I ask you again to accept my word on my answer to this "sure-kill" guy. Either this person is a relatively new

Either one of this pair of old gobblers will offer a challenge to the hunter who hunts by Gabe's rules.

The old doctor racked his
brain for a scheme to help
him kill a turkey.

turkey hunter who hasn't learned the facts of life or he is a downright liar. Over the years, I have run into some of these "sure-kill" guys. On occasions, I have taken the time to follow up on this. Without exception, when put to the field test, these guys proved to be woefully lacking in all phases of the art of turkey hunting.

Many times I have been asked, "In turkey hunting, how important is the call itself?" I have known people who won turkey calling contests and still could not consistently kill a wild turkey. I have known other people whose use of a turkey call was downright pathetic but they killed turkeys. Some people can consistently kill turkeys without the use of a turkey call. Taking all items into consideration, this is the way I rate the several factors involved in turkey hunting.

Your ability to locate a wild turkey gobbler	20%
Your expertise in approaching the located gobbler and "sitting to him."	30%
The call you make to lure the gobbler	40%
The ability to consistently make the kill when the turkey is called in range	10%
	100%

You must admit, if a person does all the above things with expertise, he will be a good turkey hunter. I have no argument with people who will disagree with my ratings of the above factors. Make up your own rating and study it. By so doing, perhaps you could improve in an area where you show a weakness.

This mother is teaching her brood, "Do lots of looking at regular intervals."

10

My Last Twenty Years

IT had been a day of one frustration after another. Early in the morning I had a fine trophy gobbler almost in gun range when a jeep-load of deer-hunters-turned-turkey-hunters almost ran over the turkey. The deer hunters never saw the turkey or me as they merrily made their way along the old logging road. After this episode, I decided to move to another area on the other side of Ponta Creek. There would be no way for a vehicle to cross this creek in this area, as the old bridge had washed away during the heavy winter rains.

I crossed Ponta Creek and the narrow fringe of trees along its banks. Parallel to the creek, a pasture lay along its side for about one-half mile. The pasture was about two hundred yards wide and contained a few cows and calves. This little pasture was the only open area for miles in any direction. It sat like an island in a sea of timbered hills and valleys. It was such a peaceful place, I decided to sit and enjoy it. I found a knoll at the creek's edge with a huge hickory tree leaning toward the creek. The hickory was on top of the knoll and, when I sat down, I had a full view of the pasture and its edges. Long ago Gabe had taught me how to sit for long periods without moving. This permits you to become a fixture and the wildlife of the area begins to circulate around you. This place reminded me of Tony McCleb's huge white oak tree that overlooked the valley of Buckatuna River. If you can find such a place, I highly recommend it for any and all the ills that might beset you. Just go to your favorite place alone and sit still and quiet and let the tranquility of the place envelop you. The hours you spend there may be the most important use you will find for your time.

I don't know how long I had been sitting in my new-found haven, but it was long enough for the actors of the area to come on stage. First off, I saw a huge swamp rabbit come bounding across the pasture full speed. I knew by the way he ran something was after him. He almost ran across my feet as he made his way to the creek. I could hear him splashing along in the edge of the water and I knew then some trailing animal was in pursuit. The rabbit was running in the edge of the creek to throw off his trail the old mother fox and her pups who also almost ran across my feet. The old fox was yapping on the rabbit's trail and each of the little foxes was following, yapping with every bound. What a sight! Later they were upstaged by wild turkeys that began to filter into the pasture. First came three turkey hens that began to pick the green grass and catch the grasshoppers and other insects. After a while two young gobblers came into the pasture and began to worry the hens constantly. I was enjoying just sitting and observing these turkeys with no thought of trying to call or kill one of the gobblers. I believe the old gobbler who finally put in his appearance had been standing in the edge of the woods for some time, observing the other turkeys. As he walked out into the pasture, a remarkable thing happened. Instead of the young gobblers running out of the pasture and away from the old gobbler, they ran to meet him. The young gobblers seemed to be trying to convince the old man that they were innocent of making any overtures toward the hens. They tried to convince him by their actions that they preferred his company to that of the hens. Mind you, I had been hunting wild turkeys for over thirty years and this was the first time for me to see this side of the wild turkey's actions and behavior. When the young gobblers got close to the old gobbler, he promptly ran each of them around in little tight circles, pecking and jumping at them. I don't believe he ever touched a one of them. Anyway, the young gobblers completely abandoned the hens and followed the old gobbler around like he was leading them with a rope. Suddenly the old gobbler took off running across the pasture like he was possessed of the devil. The young gobblers followed in close pursuit. Into the woods and out of sight they went. I was so interested in watching all this show that trying to kill any one of these gobblers never crossed my mind. After the old gobbler and the two young ones had been out of sight for about twenty minutes, the old gobbler calmly walked back into the pasture, alone. He then strutted his way to the hens and spent an hour or two showing off for their benefit. Even then I made no attempt to kill the old gobbler. I wanted to see if the young gobblers would come back. They never did and finally the hens left the pasture with his majesty trailing them.

I know a lot of people enjoy bird watching. None of them could even come close to the joy I get out of turkey watching. You now know why I deem it important to have divided my turkey career into two parts. Part one, hunting turkeys in the woods; part two, hunting and observing wild turkeys in open areas.

The time I first saw an old gobbler take over and dominate young gobblers, I thought perhaps this was unique and out of the ordinary. Not so. I have found this to be a perfectly normal relationship between old and young turkey gobblers. I have witnessed and watched it go on for hours and on at least thirty occasions. I have seen one old gobbler intimidate and lead around as many as eight young gobblers. I have seen two or more old gobblers team up and lead a bunch of young gobblers around with unbelievable discipline. I will have to say, at this point, if older people could control young people the way old gobblers control the young ones, the term 'juvenile delinquent' would not be in the dictionary.

I believe the great control adult turkeys have over younger ones is due to parental guidance, which starts when the little turkey pecks through the shell of the egg. You can readily see why this must be when you think of the tough environment in which the wild turkey is raised. For instance, say an old hen with her three-week-old poults are foraging along the edge of a clearing. The alert mother is constantly keeping a keen watch for danger from both air and land. Suddenly she sees a hawk

plummeting toward her babies who are scattered about feeding
and cavorting. The old mother gives her sharp warning cluck in
a split second. In the other part of that second, her babies
simply melt into their surroundings, even at that age, evaporat-
ing. How long do you think wild turkeys would last in the wild
if the young questioned the decisions of their elders, if they
wanted to wait and see for themselves what, if any, danger was
about or perhaps wanted mama to explain in detail why they
should seek shelter.

I have raised lots of turkeys. Some fully domesticated. Some
half wild and half tame. Some from pure wild stock. For several years I raised a large bunch of cross-bred turkeys for stock-
ing an area close to a large river in Alabama. This was a common practice about twenty years ago. Now we know better than
to introduce domestic turkey blood to wild blooded turkeys.
About fifteen tame hens crossed with full blooded wild gobblers
were used to raise the young turkeys. When a hen would hatch
off a bunch, we took the little turkeys and put them in a brooder. The hens would soon begin to lay another clutch of eggs.
When the hens sat on this last clutch of eggs and hatched them,
we let her keep the poults and raise them. Thus we had
brooder-raised young turkeys without parental guidance. From
the same mother and father, we had young turkeys who were
with their mother to be raised by her. We had planted a large
field of peas which were left in the field for the turkeys to har-
vest. When the peas ripened on the vines and were dry, the
turkeys began to feed on them. I was fascinated with the way
an old mother hen would reach up and pick a pod of peas off
the vine and drop it on the ground. Holding this pea pod with
one foot, she would then rip it open with her bill and the peas
would fly in every direction. Her poults that she had raised herself would make a scramble for these peas. Her poults that had
been taken from her and raised in a brooder wouldn't touch a
pea. Turkeys love peas. It amazed me to see this flock of
turkeys acting so differently, about one half eating and the other
half looking. Gabe Meadow once told me that little creatures
taken at a very early age and raised by man would think a man
to be his mother or parent. I thought about that and would get

down in the pea patch, pick a pea pod, and open it to try to get the brooder-raised young turkeys to partake. Nothing doing; they just looked. To this day, I am glad some of my cronies didn't catch me in the act of being a mother turkey.

This first year to cross-breed turkeys resulted in raising to maturity about fifty half-wild-blooded turkeys. I kept only the half-wild-blooded hens from the flock and had about twenty-five of them. It was my plan to again let the native wild gobblers of the area breed these half-wild hens to produce turkeys which would become three-fourths wild blooded. After this second year to thus cross-breed these turkeys, I lost control of them and they could not be handled as before. Even the first year when I had half-wild turkeys, they looked more like wild than tame turkeys. They were long-bodied, long-legged, and long-necked.

My river place where I raised these turkeys had a large population of all the native predators: wildcats, fox, owls, hawks, and people. I made no attempt to protect these turkeys even from the people who I believe were killing them every chance they got. I wanted the turkeys to find out as soon as possible who their enemies were. I hear very little mention of snakes as natural enemies of wild turkeys. These snakes, I believe, can be quite a hazard to young turkeys. Once I had twelve young half-wild turkeys in a holding pen. The turkeys were well developed, five or six weeks old. The holding pen was, I thought, predator proof. The pen had wire all around, including top and bottom. One night a big chicken snake squeezed through the wire and killed every one of these turkeys. The man I had living on the place arrived on the scene as the snake was squeezing the life out of the last little turkey. I believe the snake intended killing all the little turkeys and then swallowing all he could at his leisure.

The state of Alabama has always had good programs for protecting, restocking, and managing its wildlife. The state gave me ten adult full-blooded wild turkeys which they had pen raised. The year the state gave me these turkeys, I bought about fifteen full-blooded wild turkeys from some local people who raised them in pens as a hobby. I promptly turned all these turkeys out in the woods and most of them simply couldn't cope with the wild environment of my river place.

All this dealing in and raising turkeys brings me to one conclusion. There is simply no substitute for the wild turkey raised
in the wild by a wild mother. There are a lot of "wilds" in that
sentence and I intend it to be so. Thus, when the game man-
agers and conservation people came up with a system of trapping adult wild turkeys for transplanting, they hit the jackpot.
A pampered turkey, be he of domestic stock or wild stock, is not
the kind of turkey you want to hunt.

When I learned how much turkeys used open areas, I began
to kill quite a few turkeys around pastures, old fields, etc. Fact
is, I talked too much about it. The little pasture across Ponta
Creek became a hot spot on our club land. Brush blinds were
built by the deer hunters all around the edges. By simply sitting in these blinds, even a deer hunter could kill a turkey. The
brush blinds gave way to little houses. Some houses equipped
with a snack bar, carpeted floors, easy chairs, etc. What a
temptation these houses have become for a man as old as I am.
Out of the weather, away from insects, snakes, and the like.
Setting these "turkey houses" around pastures and old fields
has led to a new development—the clearing of food plots in
wooded areas. Now food plots are planted with foods very much
desired by turkeys. Chuffas, clovers, oats, wheat, and all kinds
of foods lure turkeys to these plots.

I am guilty of sitting in these "turkey houses" now and then.
When I have a guest who will hunt for just one or two days, the
turkey house is used. This usually lets the guest, who is not
trained to turkey hunting, get to see wild turkeys. Taking an
untrained person in the woods to try to see a turkey is extremely difficult. I have taken people like photographers to my
turkey houses to make pictures. But every time I go by myself
and sit up in a "turkey house," pangs of guilt gnaw at my conscience. I try to console my conscience by the fact that I called
the turkey up close enough to the house to kill him. Deep down
though, I know that calling wasn't necessary. Just sit and wait
for him to get in range. In this book, you will find a complete
chapter by the name of "The Turkey Hunter's Score by Degree
of Difficulty." The system I have worked out will give due

credit to the man who hunts turkeys by the time-honored, woods, one-on-one method. By the same token, those of us who take turkeys the easy way are going to pay a penalty for so doing.

I am going to take the liberty at this point to ramble about a bit. When I get turkeys on my mind, a great flood of memories crowd in, often in a jumbled kind of way, without regard for time, place, or subject matter.

I don't believe all turkey hunters will agree on any one subject pertaining to the wild turkey. That's good. It proves that the wild turkey has been, to a marked degree, successful in addling the brain of the people who pursue him with uncertainty.

I didn't always agree with master turkey hunter Gabe Meadow. As I hunted and studied turkeys, I naturally developed theories of my own. However, I found most of his beliefs and advice about the wild turkey to be good and sound. There is one piece of advice Gabe gave me that I want to share with every turkey hunter. Take my word for it, you can't possibly come by anything which will help you enjoy turkey hunting any more than this. Don't wait thirty years, as I did, to appreciate this gem. Gabe said, "Boy, you know or will learn, that this life is one great competitive melee. You have to compete to stay alive. It is good to learn to be aggressively competitive. There is one exception and you listen good to what that exception is. Don't you ever let the spirit of competition rule your actions toward killing wild turkeys. By this statement I mean don't get in a race with other hunters to kill more turkeys than them. Don't you be pushed by your ego and your reputation as a good turkey hunter to kill more turkeys than you really want to. Don't you worry about some person asking, 'how many turkeys you killed this year?' Then when you tell your score, the man will tell you about the three gobblers Joe Doe has already killed. Or the two fine gobblers Tom Tin Horn, the first year hunter, killed the first five days of the season. You will learn that the actual killing of a wild turkey is not the final gauge of your hunting success. You will learn not to give a damn who kills what or how many. You will learn to kill a few and leave a lot. You will learn to call up a fine gobbler and let him walk away.

When you conquer something, you don't necessarily have to de-
stroy it to make the victory complete. Now forget about what
other turkey hunters do and turkey hunt like you alone want to.
Sure, you'll kill a few good gobblers each year but it will be by
your own choice, not because somebody made you do it. Boy,
think on these words—some day you will appreciate them."

Wise old Gabe had put a lot of brain power behind this advice. Gabe concluded with this good advice. "When someone
pushes you for the number of turkeys you have killed this running season, tell them you only give out your score when the
season ends."

I got to thinking about old Tony McCleb's statement about the
great curiosity of the wild turkey. I vouch for that fact and have
seen many events which prove it. A transcontinental pipeline
runs across the land where I spend a lot of time with wild turkeys. This very large pipeline runs through the hills and valleys
of my favorite turkey area and the pipeline company keeps a
sixty foot right-of-way cleared of trees and bushes. Several
years ago, a leak developed in this pipeline right in the middle
of my best turkey range. At that time, natural gas was in the
pipeline and it made a hissing sound as the gas escaped out of
the ground. An employee of the pipeline company said when he
went to the place where the gas was escaping, about twenty to
twenty-five wild turkeys surrounded the leak. This man told me
several trips over a period of four days were made to the site to
repair the pipeline. Every time the workmen returned to the
leak site, the turkeys were trying to find out what was making
this hissing sound. The turkeys in the area are especially noted
for their wildness.

One advantage of hunting open areas is the opportunity to observe turkeys and their actions. Jealousy is always a big factor
in influencing the actions of males of any species. It is extremely
so where wild turkey gobblers are involved. I have used this
knowledge to kill some real trophy gobblers. The pasture I frequently hunt in is completely surrounded by woods. From my
usual place to sit at the edge of this pasture, I can see all over
it. Many times I have called up young turkeys one, two, and
even three years old and let them walk away from me. I keep

them under careful observation and, at the same time, I watch all parts of the pasture. If I see an old gobbler come into the pasture, then I call to the young gobbler who is easier to lure. When the old gobbler realizes the young gobbler is going to meet a hen, he throws caution to the wind and rushes up to get to the hen first. I killed one of my finest trophy gobblers exactly this way, after failing to take him using my entire bag of tricks. Over the years, I have taken many other fine gobblers with this tactic.

Two factors greatly influenced me as I began to like the hunting of turkeys around open areas, like pastures and old fields. Factor number one was the fact that turkeys were simply gobbling less and less as the years went by. As any turkey hunter well knows, it is extremely difficult to get up with a wild turkey gobbler in the woods unless he gobbles. Factor number two was the fact that my hearing was poor and getting poorer every year. The open space hunting allowed me to make contact with turkeys without depending on their gobbling. Hunting and just sitting and observing turkeys in open areas has brought a new dimension to my turkey knowledge. I was able to watch wild turkeys for hours and hours, week after week. Frequently I watched from morning fly-down to afternoon roost-time. During the course of this long observation, I learned things about turkeys I never knew before. In addition, I found that I had been wrong in some of my beliefs about the wild turkey.

It is my firm belief that the more knowledge you have about the wild turkey, the better turkey hunter you will be. We have established that you are playing in the big league when you turkey hunt. That being so, you manage your hunt like a manager of a big league ball team. When the game starts, every move made by your opponent and every move made by your side creates a different set of circumstances. If you are prepared properly, you will adjust to these circumstances with cool precision, not guesswork. Thus you play ball and turkey hunt by percentage. You need to know that the percentage is in your favor when you shift and make adjustments as the game progresses. As percentages go, you will lose part of the time, but most of the time you win and that is important.

I had a camphouse located right on the high banks of a large river in Alabama. The house at one time was the home of the people who owned and farmed this land. The house was rather large and consisted of several large rooms. One of the rooms overlooked the river, which was about fifty yards away. A few large trees grew between the house and the river. Early one spring season, I went over to the camp to turkey hunt for a few days. Arriving at the camphouse late at night, I turned on all the lights and unloaded my gear. I made considerable noise moving about the house, making my bed, and placing my equipment. I got up the next morning and rain was falling in sheets, driven by a strong east wind. Again I made much noise bumping around the house, preparing breakfast; and of course all the lights were turned on. I ate slowly, hoping the weather would break. After finishing breakfast, I went out on the front porch to wait out the weather. A farm road ran by the house and on down in front of it. I could see about one hundred yards down this road. Shortly after daybreak, I saw wild hen turkeys flying down out of a grove of live oaks and landing in the road. The hens were about seventy-five yards from where I sat. I watched these hens with interest as they shook themselves vigorously to rid themselves of surplus moisture. About that time, I heard a dull thud by the side of the camphouse right opposite the room where I had slept. I was amazed to see a huge gobbler had dropped out of his roost tree and was standing tall to survey the scene. Now mind you, this gobbler had roosted and I believe slept not more than thirty yards from my bed. The gobbler and I had practically slept together. Fact is, I could hardly believe it and later went out and found droppings to prove his roost tree was within thirty yards of my bed. From his perch, the gobbler was bound to have seen me as I moved about the room with the lights on.

The gobbler was watching the hens in the road and began to strut. I didn't have my gun with me, so as he turned about strutting, I eased down and crawled back into the house. I quickly picked up my gun and slipped out the back door and to the corner of the camphouse. By that time the gobbler had strutted about half way to the hens. I was kneeling by a small pecan tree and gave the gobbler five fast yelps on my diaphragm call. He pivoted and immediately retraced his route directly toward me with his wings dragging the ground. Fact is, when he got about twenty-five steps away, I halted him with a loud yelp or I believe he would have run over me. He stopped and stood tall and my 12-gauge magnum folded him like a wet rag. I believe the infidelity of this five-year-old gobbler caused his downfall. He had probably been closely associated with the five or six hens in his harem for several weeks. When this new tender maiden issued her invitation through the sweet music of her call, the old rascal just couldn't resist. The moral of this episode is: When turkey hunting in an area where turkeys are located, keep alert at all times. Turkeys have a way of showing up in unlikely places. As Gabe Meadow often said, "When dealing with a wild turkey gobbler, always expect the unexpected." I have killed many fine gobblers by taking the time to study field conditions and being alert. By the same token, I have missed a lot of turkeys by not hunting at my full capability every minute while in turkey territory. The following account also clearly illustrates why you should use your expertise to its fullest at all times.

One afternoon I was on my way to a hunting club in the hill country of West Alabama. Turkey season would open the next day and I was prepared to hunt several days. Our clubhouse sat in a small clearing about three hundred yards from a rural road. It was about an hour before sundown when I turned into the little road leading to the camphouse. I saw no vehicles had used the little camphouse road in some time, telling me that turkeys might be using the area around the clubhouse. For some reason, wild turkeys seem to like old abandoned house sites and I have found them roosting there often. Our camphouse was located on the spot where an old farmhouse once stood. I stopped my vehicle about one hundred fifty yards from the clubhouse and silently eased up the road until I could see the camphouse and the clearing which surrounded it. Taking the time to park my vehicle and slip up to the camphouse paid off, for there in the camphouse yard was a fine gobbler strutting around like he owned the place. The gobbler had several hens with him. I sat by the side of the road and watched the turkeys until night. I knew they would be roosting close to the camphouse. After dark I went back and picked up my vehicle and drove up to the camphouse. After my experience with the turkeys at the camp-house on the river, I believed these turkeys would not be disturbed by my coming in after dark. I was the only person at the club and felt I would have a good chance at this gobbler come morning. I went to bed early and was sleeping soundly when another club member arrived. This man was really a deer hunter and came in about one o'clock in the morning. I got up to greet him and we sat for a while talking. He also said he would hunt only one day as he had to go home to tend some business. I told him to choose the place he wanted to hunt as I would be able to hunt several days. He decided on an area at the far end of the club land. Now why didn't I tell him about the camphouse gobbler? Pure unadulterated selfishness, that's why. Even though I had killed scores of turkeys in the years past, the opening of each turkey season started with none. To kind of take the pressure off, I needed to kill a couple of good gobblers. The quicker the better. After that, turkey hunting be-comes extremely enjoyable and actually killing a turkey takes second place. I had not failed to kill a good bunch of turkeys each year for about forty years. Perhaps as a person gets older, he needs to prove to himself that he has not lost his turkey hunt-ing ability. The next morning turned out to be miserable, weatherwise. It was cold, windy, and drizzling rain. The other hunter and I were up real early and I wanted him to leave camp well before daylight to keep from disturbing my camphouse gob-bler. The other hunter took off before daylight for his choice place to hunt. When he left, I still had not put on my hunting clothes. So I kept on my pajamas, old bathrobe, and house shoes. The camphouse had a very large front door. I propped the front door open, which gave me a good view of the opening in front of the camphouse. I hung my camouflage jacket across the lower one-third of the doorway at about eye level. An old rocking chair was then pulled up and I would wait for daylight in solid comfort. With a good pot of coffee by my side, dry and warm, I felt guilty for hunting in such comfort.

Soon as day began to break, I started owling. I would stick my head out the doorway to owl and listen. I didn't have long to wait. The old gobbler burst forth with his shrill spine-tingling gobble. I let him gobble about four times before giving him the five fast yelps of a receptive hen. He answered with a series of three or four fast gobbles and immediately sailed off a ridge and landed right in front of the camphouse not more than thirty steps away. I was glad I had put up my camouflage jacket across the doorway. When he landed, the old turkey stood tall to survey the scene, which gave me the chance for a squeeze trigger shot at the center of his neck. I quickly retrieved the turkey as the rain was still falling in a steady drizzle. I hung the turkey on the porch and went back to bed to finish my night's sleep. It has always fascinated me to try different tactics and methods on wild turkeys. Some of the ways I had tried turned out to be miserable failures.

When the deer hunter returned to camp about nine o'clock, I was still asleep. The man was a sight to behold, wet and muddy from head to toe. When I told him what had happened, he didn't believe me. Even to this day, he doesn't believe it. I have said before, people who have only a casual knowledge of turkeys have difficulty believing some of the things I tell them about turkeys. They want me to tell them those things that happened during my fifty years of turkey hunting, but I can tell by their looks and actions, they don't believe. On the other hand, turkey hunters who have had long and close contact with the wild turkey, know by their own experiences that these events I relate are logical and true.

About four years before I killed the gobbler in the camphouse yard, an event took place I believe worth telling about. All these facts I present to you so you can think and ponder about them. Out of my fifty-three years of close observation of the wild turkey, the facts in this book are the highlights. A few of the real character wild turkeys I knew. Some of the acts and actions of wild turkeys which I think worthy of mention. Some of you who hunt wild turkeys are going to experience the very things this book tells about. Perhaps you won't be quite so shocked as I was when they happened since you will know they have happened before.

I was coaching a young fellow to turkey hunt. The spring season was about two weeks away and we were doing some preseason scouting. One of the points I had been dwelling on was the fact that a wild turkey would approach a hunter who was absolutely still and would not recognize the man. This boy and I had parked my vehicle in exactly the same place I parked the afternoon I saw the gobbler and hens in the camphouse yard. After parking, we were slowly and cautiously working our way to the camphouse. I told the boy to stay directly behind me about ten feet back. We had reached the place where we could see the camphouse and the clearing surrounding it. We stood about thirty minutes carefully studying the whole scene. It is extremely important to take plenty of time to observe a clearing, old field, or pasture. When you study turkeys you will find they feed for a while and then relax for a while. When feeding in an opening, they often move into the cover of the edges when they take a relaxing break. We saw no turkeys up to that time so we moved about half way through the opening toward the camphouse. Again we stopped to look and listen. About fifty feet from the edge of the clearing, I caught a movement and whispered to the boy to freeze. I could see several turkeys out in the woods moving around, so I gave them three fast soft yelps. I actually was in the edge of the woods but the boy was, contrary to my instructions, standing in the middle of the narrow club road. I saw this big gobbler step out of the woods into the clearing. Then another one and another, until five big old trophy gobblers were walking directly toward us. I had a little cover but the boy had absolutely none. He was standing in the middle of the road fully exposed. The gobblers began to strut and they all were in a line like a train. Every move the lead gobbler made, the others followed. They walked to within fifteen steps of us and I believe saw us all the time they were in the clearing. I could distinctly see the long sharp curved spurs on each turkey. All of them were five-year-olds or older, full breasted, long bearded. I could see the boy out of the corner of my eye and I felt sorry for him. For fully twenty minutes, these

Five big old trophy gobblers were walking directly toward us,

I bagged him in the camp-house yard. Nobody believes it.

gobblers strutted and marched around us. Not one time did they show any fear whatsoever. Finally the turkeys marched past the camphouse and out the far end of the clearing. I don't believe any other person has ever been as happy to see turkeys walk away as the boy was.

We all learn from experience and observation. The fact that the boy was out in the open and remained motionless, permitted this event to run its course without even making these five trophy gobblers suspicious. Gabe Meadow and I agreed long ago that sitting in the open woods against a big tree is the best way to sit to a turkey. Of course you have got to be still. A turkey gobbler kind of glosses over open woods and concentrates his attention on the thickets, brush piles, logs, stumps, and other places offering cover to predators. A wildcat doesn't have enough savvy to sit motionless in front of a tree; a man does. The boy was so shaken by the ordeal, we stopped at the camphouse to relax. The boy had never killed a turkey and had seen only one or two during his two years to hunt. Perhaps this experience helped the boy because he developed into a pretty good turkey hunter.

During these last twenty years and the population explosion of turkeys, killing a turkey just "ain't what it used to be." Fact is, I would gladly swap any one of my last twenty-three years for any one of my first twenty years to hunt. I will never forget the hard-earned turkeys of the first thirty-three years. Actually I hunted ten times as hard then as now to kill a turkey. During the last fifteen years, turkeys are so plentiful they often travel in unbelievable droves. I see and hear of droves of young gobblers having six to fifteen turkeys. Old gobblers are seen having up to eleven to the drove. I shudder to think what may happen when a drove of eight young gobblers walk through a food plot and up to a turkey house containing a couple of people with automatic shotguns. Perhpas these two hunters have never even seen a wild turkey before. Maybe the hunters have been placed in the turkey house before daylight by a host who has lots of food plots with turkey houses on each. The hunters may have been told to kill only gobblers. The eight turkeys coming down through the food plot feeding on the tender clover and grass are making their living the easy way. The hunters in the house are going to kill their turkeys the easy way. The hunters determine that all these turkeys are gobblers when they see the little beards dangling in the morning sun. When more than one old gobbler approaches a hunter, on rare occasions, the surviving gobbler or gobblers may become rattled and confused when the companion is killed. Most of the time young turkeys would become so rattled and confused at the shot being fired into their midst by persons unseen that they would become easy marks for the person to kill them also. Of course, not all people would take advantage of a situation like this. There are lots of good sportsmen. However, there always have to be a few who would, and those are the ones I worry about. As I point out, these two people who have never seen a wild turkey could kill two to six of these turkeys easily. Perhaps they could kill all eight if they so desired.

Now let's take these two people and the eight young gobblers and put them in a different setting. The two hunters and the eight young gobblers are in the woods. There are no food plots or fixed blinds, no turkey houses with chairs and little portholes to shoot out of. These two men, without experience or training in the ways of wild turkeys, are trying to make contact with the eight young gobblers. If the men hunted twenty days, they would be lucky if each of them caught a fleeting look at even one of these turkeys. Neither of the men would come close to getting a shot at a turkey.

My home town here in Mississippi has a fine Junior College. The college has a program called "continuing adult education." Night classes are held for people who want to further their education. In addition to the usual subjects taught in schools, this Junior College will conduct classes in almost any subject, provided enough people agree to attend the class. A nominal fee is charged the student. I was approached by the college to see if I would teach a class on "Hunting The Wild Turkey." This kind of flabbergasted me as I, up to this point, knew nothing about the great variety of subjects taught at this college. Since I didn't get to attend college, I have always been somewhat awed by colleges and the people who run them. I went out to the college to talk it over with them. I was impressed by the great variety of subjects being taught and by the people who did the teaching. Mostly the teachers were professional people from every sort of profession and trade. I told them I would think it over and let them know. After much thought, I decided to give it a try. The college announced the class would be held and the registrations poured in. Enough people registered for two classes or about eighty people. We decided to conduct only one class of forty and take the first forty to register. It is amazing what my love for wild turkeys has gotten me in to. I thought, here I am a college professor and the wild turkey is responsible for it.

My college class was a new and rewarding experience. Every Tuesday night for six weeks we held sessions of three hours each. That's eighteen hours of turkey talk. We had people commute from surrounding towns to attend the class. The reason I decided to try to teach this class about the wild turkey is the same reason I try to write this book. I am sure most people who came to my class figured to learn "how to kill a wild turkey." Perhaps most people who read this book do so with the thought "it might help me kill a wild turkey." I believe people who attended the class and the readers of this book will be better turkey hunters. However, if learning to kill a turkey is all my class and readers have learned, then I have failed, miserably, as a teacher and a writer. One of my older students, a good turkey hunter in his own right, summed it up when he said to me, "Gene, these people came to your class to learn to kill a wild turkey and you have taught them to love the wild turkey." I told this man the philosophy I passed on to the class wasn't really mine in the first place. I have just been carrying it around for a while for some people I once knew. I don't feel that I have fulfilled my obligation to the fullest but I'm still trying. My criteria for judging the success of my "passing it on" is simply this. To have a person I have taught wild turkey lore call up a big old gobbler, after weeks of trying to do so, and let the gobbler walk away to pass his genes to the wild turkey of tomorrow. As Gabe Meadow said, "you let a few of the real smart turkeys live, when the power is in your hands, then you can aptly be called 'A Turkey Man'.''

Gabe Meadow, Kyle Delk, and Tony McCleb are all gone. The world is a better place for their having lived in it. Each of them made a great contribution to the art of hunting the wild turkey. Each of them learned how to get the maximum enjoyment out of hunting the wild turkey. Each one of them was a master turkey hunter. Each was a turkey man. Each was an old pro.

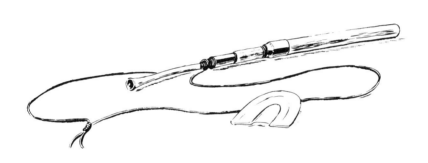

You have bagged your turkey.
Now work up your score as
set forth in this chapter 11.

11

The Turkey Hunter's Score by
Degree of Difficulty

A PHENOMENON of the highest rank. The remarkable come-back of the wild turkey. The explosion of the wild turkey pop-ulation. The waves of new hunters to the sport of wild turkey hunting. The publicity given the hunting of the wild turkey by the Outdoor Magazines and other media. The turkey calling contests. The rise and rapid growth of the Wild Turkey Fed-eration. The dedication of many organizations, including the Wild Turkey Federation, to the welfare of the wild turkey.

All fantastic and unbelievable. But where do we go from here?

It is our great desire that some people who read our book will gain a new look at the wild turkey. We hope some will accept the real challenge a wild turkey offers the hunter when the tur-key is hunted properly. We sincerely believe the wild turkey survived in this country because a small band of dedicated tur-key hunters insisted that the wild turkey be hunted properly. When we started hunting wild turkeys along about 1925, many people were saying the wild turkey would go the way the pas-senger pigeon went—out of existence. When we got to know real turkey men like Gabe Meadow, Kyle Delk, and Tony Mc-Cleb, we knew the wild turkey was going to make it. These great men and others like them simply stood between the would-be turkey exterminators and the wild turkey until the forces of conservation and law enforcement came to the rescue.

After much thought, we have worked out a formula to evaluate the turkey hunter's expertise in hunting and bagging a wild turkey. It has been a most difficult task to say the least. We have tried to be fair with the man who hunts wild turkeys in a state with a limited turkey population, a very short season, and a season bag limit of one. His point total reflects the short season and small bag limit through a larger credit for, in effect, killing his limit within the short season. By the same token, a hunter from a state with a twenty-one day or longer season and a bag limit of several turkeys receives less credit per turkey.

People who are dedicated to the proper hunting of the wild turkey should be greatly concerned about the turn of events of recent years. We greatly fear the ease of killing a wild turkey today is going to bring hordes of people to the sport. Who is going to teach these people to appreciate the wild turkey and his challenge to a hunter? Who is going to teach this young novice hunter the unique and rewarding experience of properly hunting the wild turkey? Should we show this young hunter that even the native Indian of America recognized the challenge the wild turkey offered? Earlier in this book we quoted from the writings of an English author of the early 1700s. Again we quote, "savage man seems to find a delight in precarious possession. A great part of the pleasure of the chase lies in the uncertainty of the pursuit. Hunting the wild turkey makes one of the Indians' principal diversions." We never really looked at hunting turkeys that way. The more we have thought about it, the more we realize that the "uncertainty of the pursuit" is in fact the crux of wild turkey hunting. Every turkey hunter knows, when we remove this uncertainty of the pursuit, the hunt could become boring and downright routine. When you bait turkeys, you most certainly will remove the "uncertainty" factor. When you sit in a turkey house on a lush food plot, the uncertainty factor is gone. Your grandmother could, under these conditions, kill a wild turkey as easily as you. I will fuss no more about these weaknesses of men.

How well I remember the many people who in the years past would take up turkey hunting and after a year or two of hardship and frustration would throw up their hands and quit. A little ditty Old Tony McCleb sang to me as a boy kind of tells of the old days. How a man takes up turkey hunting—fails and quits.

> Twenty-eight days
> And what do I get?
>
> Not a durn feather
> And a wife to fret
>
> I'm gonna hang my musket
> On the wall
>
> And give these turkeys
> My very last call

Years ago I knew a man who hunted wild turkeys each spring for twenty years without killing one. This same man hunting by some of today's methods could easily kill a turkey within the first two days. He could also kill another turkey every few days throughout the season.

Study carefully my method of scoring the turkey hunter's success. Set your sights a little higher. Endeavor to raise your score by giving the wild turkey a fair chance. You'll be glad you did and the very survival of the wild turkey could be at stake.

Toward the end of this chapter you will find paragraphs which outline my method of scoring. Each of these paragraphs begins with the word "Factor" followed by a number. Example: Factor No. 1, Factor No. 2, Factor No. 3, etc., etc. You will note there are a total of twenty-two factors.

You will find most of these factors are relative to any turkey you kill. Some factors, however, may not relate to you, your turkey, or the conditions under which you killed your turkey. Example: Factor No. 22 assesses a penalty of minus one hundred points for any violation of the law in the killing of your turkey. If your kill was legal, then factor twenty-two is left blank on the score sheet as it does not apply to you.

These factors and the points given at the end of each, determine your final score. You will note a number of factors give plus points. Also there are factors which give minus points. All the plus points are added together and all the minus points, if any, are added together. When you subtract the total of all minus points from the total of all plus points, the remaining figure is your final score. In some extreme cases, it is possible to wind up with a final *minus score.*

The plus points earned by certain factors reflect your expertise and your sportsmanship. Also you earn plus points for conditions existing in your hunting area that handicap you in competing with turkey hunters from other areas. These handicaps, to name a few, are: small wild turkey population of your area, small bag limit of your area, and short open season to hunt. It is our aim to put the turkey hunter from a state with the above handicaps on a near equal basis with turkey hunters from states having more wild turkeys, longer hunting seasons, and larger bag limits. My whole system of scoring covers the spring turkey seasons. To some degree, however, the system would apply to fall or other seasons.

The minus points assessed against the hunter reflect field conditions, some natural, some artificial, which make it easier to kill a wild turkey. We don't penalize too severely a hunter who kills a pen-raised wild turkey, a mere minus twenty points. By the same token we do assess a heavy penalty for killing a wild turkey over bait, a stiff, minus fifty points.

Each factor is listed below by number. Following the factor number is an explanation of the factor and our reason for making it a plus or minus. I know no other turkey hunter is going to agree 100% with my method of scoring. If you don't agree, take heart, because I don't either, not completely. Fact is, I juggled the figures so much I wore out all the erasers on hand; so finally I had to accept the ones you see.

The outdoor magazines, newspapers, and other media contain many stories about turkey hunting due to the surge of popularity of the sport. After reading one of the stories, you can now score that hunter's expertise and evaluate his method of hunting. Of course, you will want to work up your own score on every turkey you kill.

If your score is 425 points or over for three consecutive years, I pronounce you an "expert turkey hunter."

If your score is 425 points or over for five consecutive years, I pronounce you a "master turkey hunter."

If you recall, with certainty, the turkeys you have killed over the past five years you may figure your score, including them. This will permit a hunter to reach the "expert" or "master" status more quickly.

All of the following factors apply to each turkey you kill during a calendar year.

FACTOR NUMBER 1—BEARDS

Each 1" of beard length earns three (3) points. If you are lucky and your turkey had more than one distinct beard, combine the lengths of all the beards and multiply by three (3). The turkey's beard continues to grow during his lifetime, there is a continuous wearing off and breaking off of the beard at its end. The wearing and breaking off of the beard thus limits it to about twelve inches in length as a maximum. Examples: a 12" beard earns 12 x 3 = 36 points; a 4" beard earns 4 x 3 = 12 points, etc.

FACTOR NUMBER 2—SPURS

Each 1/16" of spur length earns two (2) points. The spur of only one leg qualifies. Spurs are usually considered by most turkey hunters to be the best guide to the age of a turkey. The longer the spurs, the older the turkey. The older the turkey, the smarter he becomes and the more challenging he is to kill. Spurs continue to grow during the life of a wild turkey and tend to get sharper as he ages. The spurs also tend to curve as they approach their maximum length. Spurs of one inch (1") or longer are considered approaching trophy status. Example:

spurs 1/2 inch long equals 8/16" and 8 x 2 = 16 points, 3/4" long equals 12/16" and 12 x 2 = 24 points, spurs 1" long equals 16/16" and 16 x 2 = 32 points, etc. The best set of spurs I have are 1 7/16 inches long which equals 23/16" and 23 x 2 = 46 points.

FACTOR NUMBER 3—WEIGHT

Each one (1) pound of weight earns two (2) points. Perhaps this factor will benefit some of the hunters in areas outside the southeast. From the stories I read and the conversations with hunters in other parts of the country, their turkeys frequently weigh in the twenties (20s). In our southeast, an eighteen (18) pound wild turkey is a good one. According to the weight factor, these examples apply: a twelve pound (12 lb.) turkey earns 12 x 2 = 24 plus points, a sixteen pound (16 lb.) turkey earns 16 x 2 = 32 plus points, an eighteen pound (18 lb.) turkey earns 18 x 2 = 36 points, etc.

FACTOR NUMBER 4

Some states raise wild-blooded turkeys and release them at certain times to be hunted. Some private clubs also follow this practice. This, of course, beats having no wild turkeys at all to hunt. The pen-raised man-aided turkeys, even though they be pure wild-blooded, just don't offer the ultimate challenge of wild turkeys raised in the wild by a wild mother. We don't penalize the hunters of such turkeys too severely.

If you killed a pen-raised wild-blooded turkey, your score is minus 20 points.

FACTOR NUMBER 5

It is illegal to kill a hen turkey in the areas I hunt in Mississippi and Alabama. Some areas and states do permit the killing of hens. In my opinion hens offer little or no challenge to the hunter. It is not my desire to pass judgment on the right or wrong of the act. I will not kill a hen turkey regardless of the legal status of so doing. I am not going to penalize a person killing a hen turkey.

However, in deference to my old friends and master turkey hunters who all felt so strongly against the killing of hens, I will simply say, if the turkey you killed is a gobbler, your score is plus 20 points.

FACTOR NUMBER 6

The longer turkeys are raised out in the wild by wild mothers, the wilder they become up to a point. We believe five years to be sufficient to produce a good wild turkey.

If your turkey came from an area where wild turkeys have been raised in the wild for five years or longer, your score is plus 20 points.

FACTOR NUMBER 7

This factor may seem to be somewhat of a duplicate of factor six. There is a big difference, as I will explain. Factor six deals with the turkey being raised in the wild, which does not necessarily include being hunted. The wild turkey's greatest enemy is man. A turkey may be good and wild but not to the degree he will become after man puts hunting pressure on him. Continuous hunting pressure—the life and death struggle between turkey and man—hones the turkey wildness to its peak. This factor credits the hunter for killing a turkey in hunting pressure areas.

Hunting pressure in area up through three years plus 10 points.

Hunting pressure in area up through six years plus 15 points.

Hunting pressure in area longer than six years plus 20 points.

FACTOR NUMBER 8

The length of turkey seasons in a hunter's area is, of course, extremely important. Some areas allow a hunter to hunt up to seven times as long as in other areas. Having more hunting time in his area gives the hunter an opportunity to pick ideal weather and cope with other conditions. Also, the longer season allows the hunter to spend more time in the field and increases his chance for success. This factor by its large point difference reflects the importance of the season's length.

Less than ten-day turkey season earns pluss 100 points.

Ten- through twenty-day turkey season earns plus 50 points.

Longer than twenty-day turkey season earns plus 10 points.

FACTOR NUMBER 9

Wild turkey populations in the United States vary tremendously from state to state. A hunter's chance of success is, of course, much greater in states with large numbers of wild turkeys. This factor nine adjusts the hunter's score by giving the turkey hunter in thinly populated states due credit for this condition. The wild turkey population of your state earns plus points as shown.

Wild turkey population up through 12,000 earns 100 plus points.

Wild turkey population 12,001 through 25,000 earns 50 plus points.

Wild turkey populations 25,001 through 50,000 earns 25 plus points.

Wild turkey populations over 50,001 earns 10 plus points. See page 136 for wild turkey population by states.

FACTOR NUMBER 10

Turkey houses are permanent fixed blinds usually located on or near food plots. They are usually left on location all year round. Some are elaborate with snack bar and easy chairs. All have small slots or windows so the hunter can observe or shoot turkeys with comfort and ease. I know a lot of turkeys are killed from these fixed turkey houses. Many of the hunters killing turkeys this way would have a hard time killing a turkey out in the woods with call and gun—one on one. If you choose this easy method of hunting wild turkeys, you must pay a penalty.

If you killed your turkey from a fixed blind or turkey house, your score is minus 30 points.

FACTOR NUMBER 11

The clearing and planting of food plots in wooded areas is becoming popular as a practice to attract and hold wild turkeys in an area. Planted foods like chufas, oats, wheat, clover, etc., will cause the wild turkey to come to these plots to feed and loaf. Turkeys like openings like these even if not planted with foods. We class food plots an artificial aid and they make the killing of a turkey much easier.

If your turkey was killed on or near a food plot, your score is minus 30 points.

FACTOR NUMBER 12

The number of wild turkeys a hunter can legally kill per season is a tremendous item in building up a good score. The season's limit in one state may be one and another state five. We try to adjust the scoring to the fact that a good turkey hunter could kill his area's limit of wild turkeys, be it one or five.

If your area's bag limit is 1 turkey, score plus 100 points.

If your area's bag limit is 2 turkeys, score plus 50 points.

If your area's bag limit is 3 turkeys, score plus 30 points.

If your area's bag limit is 4 turkeys or more, score plus 15 points.

FACTOR NUMBER 13

Bow hunting is growing as a sport. Some bow hunters are killing wild turkeys with bow and arrow. Some hunters are killing wild turkeys with scope rifles. It seems to us these are the extremes. One hunter accepts the ultimate challenge, the other the easiest way. We merely say the one who adds to the uncertainty of the pursuit by hunting the wild turkey with bow and arrow is going to be gratified and rewarded when he takes his turkey this way.

If you kill your turkey with bow and arrow, you earn
a plus 40 points.

FACTOR NUMBER 14

We believe man has enough things going for him in his attempts to kill a wild turkey. Today's turkey hunter has the advantage of modern methods and equipment. The hunter has powerful four-wheel-drive vehicles to carry him into the remotest areas. He has powerful magnum shotguns and ammunition, camouflage clothes, good insecticides, more turkeys, longer seasons, and many more things in his favor. The wild turkey has to make do with about the same equipment he had hundreds of years ago. Some states now outlaw the use of rifles for turkey hunting. We don't believe a hunter needs a rifle in turkey hunting and assess a penalty for the use of a rifle.

If you killed your turkey with an open-sight rifle, minus
20 points.
If you killed your turkey with a scoped rifle, minus
40 points.

FACTOR NUMBER 15

People who have hunted and studied the wild turkey know him to be radically different from all other creatures on this earth. So different, in fact that he is in a class by himself. However, in spite of this great difference, he shares with all the other creatures one common trait. He will pursue the course of least resistance. He will not dig, scratch, and search for food if you hand it to him. Put corn in his path and he will lose his independence, his wildness, his lean powerful physique, and his life itself. The wisest old gobbler in an area can be killed by the area's poorest hunter with bait.

If bait or grain was within two hundred yards of the kill site, the penalty is minus 50 points.

FACTOR NUMBER 16

We have mixed emotions about people who band together to hunt wild turkeys. It is true that numbers of people still believe that the one-on-one, one hunter one turkey, is the best and most challenging way. To get the maximum enjoyment out of hunting the wild turkey, we believe a hunter should learn to do it all. He should learn to locate his turkey, call his turkey, and finally make the kill.

If another person aided you in locating, calling, or killing your turkey, your score is minus 20 points.

FACTOR NUMBER 17

During your contact with the gobbler you killed, did he gobble? If he did gobble, you are going to receive credit for having made contact with a gobbling turkey. We believe this is going to work in favor of people hunting in states having only recently opened seasons on wild turkeys. Our theory of turkeys gobbling less in areas which have been hunted hard and continuously is explained in this book. We believe it.

If your turkey gobbled during your confrontation with him, your score is plus 15 points.

FACTOR NUMBER 18

This factor deals with a delicate and controversial issue. Where was the turkey when you shot him? On the ground, in the air, or in a tree? We believe there are proper ways to hunt and kill a wild turkey. It is proper to shoot doves and quail in the air, not on the ground. It is proper to shoot a wild turkey on the ground, not in the air or in a tree. Our reasons for these penalties for wing shooting or tree shooting a wild turkey are simple. Shooting turkeys on the wing often results in the killing of hen turkeys which in our book is a no no. In addition, wing shooting of turkeys is bound to produce a high percent of wounded birds and the wild turkey deserves a better fate than that. As for shooting a turkey in a tree, we assess a still stiffer penalty. When a turkey is killed in a tree we figure, most times, it is roost shooting pure and simple. Due to the disagreements this factor will bring, the plus and minus points are relatively small. This is in deference to those who disagree with us.

When you killed your turkey:
The turkey was on the ground—score is plus 5 points.
The turkey was in the air—score is minus 10 points.
The turkey was in a tree—score is minus 20 points.

FACTOR NUMBER 19

Wild turkeys like to roost over water, along streams, sloughs, and lakes, and a lot of them are killed as a result. It is relatively easy to glide a boat silently under a roosting turkey. We have seen some well-made floating blinds built for this purpose.

If you killed your turkey from a boat or floating blind—
score is minus 40 points.

FACTOR NUMBER 20

We guess most creatures on this earth have what they consider home. Home would include the place you sleep and the place you spend most of your time when awake. At times natural disasters will force man and other creatures from their natural homes. In the case of wild turkeys, floods often force them out of their natural habitat. Heavy timber cutting, road building, and other acts of man can also force turkeys out of their usual range. Thus a wild turkey forced into strange surroundings is put at somewhat of a disadvantage.

If the turkey you killed was forced from his natural habitat, your score is minus 20 points.

FACTOR NUMBER 21

It is amazing that the wild turkey population is growing by leaps and bounds and this growth right along with the people population growth. In the old days there were probably wild turkeys who never saw a man. We don't believe this is true today. Fact is, we know of turkeys who raise wild within plain view of national super highways. Cars, buses, and trucks don't seem to bother them. On farms and ranches, the farmer's tractors and trucks are tolerated by wild turkeys when no hunting is allowed from them. This same trust that the turkey puts in the farmer's vehicles makes the poor turkey vulnerable to those who would shoot him from a vehicle. We have suggested to farmers and ranchers that they not let their wild turkeys become complacent around farm vehicles. If necessary, shots should be fired over the heads of the turkeys and the driver should jump out of the vehicle running and shouting at the turkeys to scare the daylight out of them. Riding the roads and killing turkeys from them seems to be the way to hunt turkeys for some people. We don't believe the wild turkey deserves this kind of treatment.

If your turkey was killed from a wheeled or motor-powered vehicle, your score is minus 40 points.

FACTOR NUMBER 22

Most of the factors giving plus points in our turkey scoring system award the hunter for giving the turkey a fair chance. Most of our factors which assess minus points do so because of our disapproval of the way the turkey is hunted and killed. We don't think any of our factors which give the hunter plus points would cover illegal acts. Some of the factors assessing a penalty of minus points are illegal in some states. This factor twenty-two simply penalizes a person who violates a law; hunting out of season, over the bag limit, trespassing and other illegal acts. In some cases, this could lead to double jeopardy, like killing a turkey over bait in Alabama. Under factor twelve, you would be penalized a minus fifty points and under this factor twenty-two again penalized minus one hundred points. We believe it is good that this is so.

If any acts of yours in killing your turkey was against the law, your score is minus 100 points.

SPECIAL CONSIDERATION

After reviewing all twenty-two factors and working up scores on many, many turkeys killed under all kinds of circumstances, there seems to be something missing. What about the most dedicated turkey hunter of all? The hunter who calls up and lets a fine turkey gobbler live. He who has fulfilled this book's portrayal of the turkey man supreme. Here and now we are correcting this oversight.

A turkey hunter calls up, within shotgun range, a mature turkey gobbler. There is no doubt the turkey's life is but a trigger pull away. The turkey has been called to the site without the aid of bait, other hunters, or any type of decoy. This is truly the classical one-on-one hunting of the wild turkey. For each mature turkey gobbler thus called to the gun during a single year, add two hundred points to your score. As you will realize, it is possible to qualify as an expert or master turkey hunter without spilling a drop of blood. So be it.

THE TURKEY HUNTER'S SCORE BY DEGREE OF DIFFICULTY

Factor No.		Plus Points	Minus Points
1	Each 1'' of beard length earns	Plus 3 Points	
2	Each 1/16'' of spur length earns	Plus 2 Points	
3	Each 1 lb. of weight (undressed) earns	Plus 2 Points	
4	If your turkey was pen raised, a penalty of	Minus 20 Points	
5	If your turkey is a gobbler, he earns	Plus 20 Points	
6	If your turkey was raised in the wild for five (5) years or longer, he earns	Plus 20 Points	
7	The years of hunting pressure in an area earns plus points Yrs. of pressure/plus points—thru 3 Yrs./10 Pts. thru 6 Yrs./15 Pts.—more than 6 Yrs./20 Pts.		

Factor No.		Plus Points	Minus Points

8   The length of season to hunt turkeys in your area earns plus points. Less than 10 days/100 Pts.—10 thru 20 days/50 Pts.—longer than 20 days/10 Pts.

9   The population of wild turkeys in your state earns plus Pts. Up thru 12,000/100 Pts.—12,001 thru 25,000/50 Pts. —25,001 thru 50,000/25 Pts.—over 50,001/10 Pts.

10   If your turkey was killed from a fixed blind or turkey house, penalty   Minus 30 Points

11   If your turkey was killed on or near a food plot, penalty   Minus 30 Points

12   Plus points are earned according to the legal bag limit of your area. Limit/plus Pts. 1/100 Pts.—2/50 Pts. —3/30 Pts.—4 or more/15 Pts.

13   Turkeys killed with bow and arrow earns   Plus 40 Points

14   Rifle killing of turkeys will penalize the hunter.
Use of open-sight rifles   Minus 20 Points
Scoped rifles   Minus 40 Points

15   If bait or grain was within two hundred yards of the kill site, the penalty is   Minus 50 Points

16   If another person aided you in locating, calling, or killing your turkey, the penalty is   Minus 20 Points

17   If your turkey gobbled during your confrontation with him, this fact earns a   Plus 15 Points

18   If your turkey was on the ground when killed, this earns   Plus 5 Points
If your turkey was in the air when killed, penalty is   Minus 10 Points
If your turkey was in a tree when killed, penalty is   Minus 20 Points

19   If you killed your turkey from a boat or floating blind, the penalty is   Minus 40 Points

20   If the turkey you killed was forced out of his natural habitat by floods, road building, etc., the penalty is   Minus 20 Points

21   If your turkey was killed from a wheeled or motor-powered vehicle other than a boat, the penalty is   Minus 40 Points

22   If any act of yours in taking your turkey was in violation of the law, the penalty is   Minus 100 Points

Add all plus points and add all minus points; put totals here. Subtract the total of all minus points from the total of all plus points and your final score is,

Plus points   less minus points   equals

             Final Score.

ESTIMATED WILD TURKEY POPULATIONS 1978 BY STATES

Alabama	300,000	Nebraska	6,000
Arizona	40,000	New Mexico	20,000
Arkansas	50,000	New York	14,000
California	10,000	North Carolina	5,000
Colorado	12,000	North Dakota	3,500
Florida	80,000	Ohio	4,000
Georgia	20,000	Oklahoma	30,000
Hawaii	2,000	Oregon	2,000
Idaho	1,000	Pennsylvania	100,000
Illinois	2,000	South Carolina	15,000
Indiana	3,000	South Dakota	6,000
Kansas	2,000	Tennessee	8,000
Kentucky	2,000	Texas	400,000
Louisiana	15,000	Utah	2,000
Maryland	2,000	Vermont	8,000
Michigan	6,000	Virginia	50,000
Mississippi	100,000	Washington	2,000
Missouri	60,000	West Virginia	25,000
Montana	6,000	Wyoming	10,000

12

The Wrap Up

WHEN a person takes up turkey hunting, perhaps the first thing that comes to mind is to get a turkey call and learn to use it. That sounds simple enough but it is one of the most controversial of all the subjects related to hunting the wild turkey. We will separate the callers or devices from the sounds they produce in order to help the new hunter achieve his objective one step at a time.

Wild turkeys have a tremendous vocabulary. The sounds they make cover a very wide range and when you add the variety of tone, pitch, volume, rhythm, and inflection to these sounds, the scope is seemingly endless. I believe it is unlikely that the average turkey hunter would be able to hear all these sounds and to identify them even over a lifetime of hunting. Forget all these sounds. You are starting to hunt wild turkeys, not preparing for the national wild turkey calling championship. At first you will need to concentrate on making only the simple basic sounds— only one call or at most two at this stage.

By all means go to your sporting goods store and buy a good record or cassette on turkey calling even before you buy a turkey call. If your sporting goods store doesn't have them in stock you can order them direct from the experts who make them. I recommend the following as being among the best you can buy:

RECORDS AND CASSETTES BY:

Jack Dudley—World Champion Caller
Dekalb, MS 39328

Ben Rodgers Lee—World Champion Caller
Coffeeville, AL 36524

Old Pro Products—Old Pro Turkey Man
P. O. Box 1190
Meridian, MS 39301

After you have bought the record or cassette, you then get off to yourself so that, without interruption, you can listen over and over to this turkey talk. Remember the people who are making all these turkey sounds were once exactly where you are at this moment. They had to start from scratch like you. It must be said that these expert turkey callers were willing to spend long hours over many years to perfect these wild turkey sounds.

Every good record and cassette will include the one basic call which at this stage is the call you will concentrate on. This call is the mating call of the wild turkey hen. It is one of the easiest of all calls to make. This mating call is a soft rapid series of yelps. Three, four, or five of these yelps, ke-ouk - ke-ouk - ke-ouk are all you need to lure a gobbler. If you could learn but one call, this would be the one. In the spring this mating call is the most effective sound you can make and it has probably called more turkey gobblers to the gun than all other calls combined. You now know the sound you want to make and your next step is to buy a turkey call.

The population explosion of the wild turkey has created a big demand for turkey calls. To fill this demand, many people and firms are making them. Most every store that handles sporting goods will have turkey calls for sale. For the new hunter, I recommend that he start with some type of box call or friction-type call. Have the salesperson at the store demonstrate the call. You have fixed in your mind the sounds you want to make from listening to the records or cassettes. My reason for your starting with the box call is because it is the easiest to learn to use. Eventually, however, as your calling improves and you perhaps kill a turkey or two, you will by all means want to step up to the diaphragm call. The diaphragm call is to turkey hunting what the plastic worm is to fishing. The plastic worm catches fish and the diaphragm turkey call will call turkeys—both of these produce and no person will argue with that.

Actually, the use of the diaphragm-type call is very old—the principle has been used for perhaps more than a hundred years. How well I remember an old turkey hunter named Slim Doss who lived down the road from our rural home; I was about six years old and would go to Slim's house in early spring to hear him practice turkey calling. He would take a green leaf from a briar or wild cherry or dogwood and hold it to his lips and produce essentially the same sounds we get out of the modern diaphragm. Other old hunters would take thin strips of rubber which they stretched between their lips to produce the sounds they desired. Many of these old hunters were quite good callers using the leaf or rubber strips. It naturally followed that some ingenious person would think of a device for holding the diaphragm in a fixed manner to use this call more easily.

If you want to begin with the diaphragm, that's OK. But prepare to spend lots of time learning to use it. In the beginning I told you to learn to make one sound or call at a time. After you have learned to make the mating call of the turkey hen you can move on to other sounds. Learning to make the all important yelp, the ke-ouk, ke-ouk, ke-ouk of the wild turkey gives you the basic sound from which you can branch off easily to other calls. To move into the fall calling of a scattered drove of wild turkeys, you use the yelp you have learned to make but you make the call much louder and longer. Instead of the three to five soft yelps you now make eight to ten yelps about twice as loud and much slower. At the end of your series of slow yelps, occasionally add four or five fast loud yelps. You are making the lost call of the wild turkey and this call is basic to fall hunting. For many years I had the choice to hunt wild turkeys both in the fall and spring. I was never able to enjoy the fall hunting like spring. To me the fall hunting simply didn't offer the challenge and enjoyment of the spring season. I was therefore not willing to use up my bag limit or any part of it on fall gobblers. If you have the chance to hunt wild turkeys both spring and fall, I suggest you try both to see which appeals to you.

My book covers primarily the spring hunting of the wild turkey. A good spring turkey hunter would also be able to kill turkeys in the fall. Knowledge and understanding of the wild turkey is your best asset and a turkey is the same, year round. Slight changes in technique and calling is all you need to switch from spring to fall.

If you have followed my advice you are ready to buy your turkey call. As stated there are many to choose from, as there are literally hundreds on the market. I will make no attempt to list them all but will simply list a few of the ones I consider among the best.

FRICTION OR BOX-TYPE CALLS MANUFACTURED BY:

Ben Rodgers Lee
Coffeeville, AL 36524

M. L. Lynch Company
Liberty, MS 39645

Sidney W. Vaughn
Rt. 4
Grenada, MS

DIAPHRAGM OR MOUTH-TYPE CALLS MANUFACTURED BY:

Ben Rodgers Lee
Coffeeville, AL 36524

P. S. Olt Company
Pekin, IL 61554

Penn's Woods Products
Delmont, PA 15626

One of the finest aids to turkey hunting each year will be your annual check list of equipment and supplies. We made up our list about thirty years ago and it has given us peace of mind since that time. Your own list will be different as your needs will not be exactly the same as other turkey hunters. The most frustrating thing that can happen to a turkey hunter is to arrive at his favorite hunting spot and then discover some important item missing. My list consists of about fifty items. I took a large cardboard and drew ten vertical lines the entire length of the card, making ten columns. In the first column I listed the items of equipment. In the other

CHECK LIST OF TURKEY HUNTING EQUIPMENT

Item	1975	1976	1977	1978	1979	1980	1981	1982	1983
Gun									
Ammo									
Calls									
Boots									
Clothes									
Flashlight									
Insecticide									
Compass									
Etc.									

columns I listed the years I used the check list. By so doing it is very simple to check the list at the start of the turkey season each year. I have an arrangement with my family by which a space is set aside for all the equipment. It stays in one place during the entire turkey season. Every item I will use during the whole season is there in full view and it is easy to pick up the equipment you need for each specific hunt.

One of my best pieces of equipment is a homemade combination blind, raincape, seat, and multipurpose item. I purchased twenty-four feet of lightweight camouflage material four feet wide. I then bought a piece of polyethylene film four mils thick by twelve feet long by four feet wide. I laid the camouflage material on a smooth surface and then put the polyethylene material on top of it at one end. By folding over the other end of the camouflage material, you have camo material on both sides of the poly material in a sandwich arrangement. The camouflage material can be sewed around the edges or secured by a good waterproof adhesive. This gives you a fine lightweight waterproof cover four feet wide and twelve feet long. At all corners tie about five feet of nylon cord. This cover can be rolled or folded into a compact package for easy carrying. Items you want to keep dry can be wrapped in it. It makes a fine blind quickly. It will keep you dry for hours. If you get cold, wrap up in it. Use it to sit on wet ground. I carry it in my turkey mac back game pocket and it supports the small of my back when I sit in front of a large tree slumped down with knees drawn up in front. At this point I would like to recommend the turkey mac game vest as the best I have found for carrying all your turkey hunting accessories. It is designed for turkey hunters and fills the need nicely. The turkey mac is made of good material and has plenty of deep pockets. Mr. Albert McMillan, Sr. of Morton, Mississippi, a real wild turkey buff, designed this game vest for turkey hunters. It could be bought direct from Mr. McMillan. You can order a catalogue of turkey hunting aids, including call and records, from Ben Lee, Coffeeville, AL 36524. The equipment Ben Lee makes or has made for him is in my opinion the best you can buy.

Your choice of gun and ammunition for turkey hunting must be made. The magnum 12-gauge shotgun and the three-inch shells are considered best for turkey hunting. After years and years of shooting size six (6) shot I have switched to size four (4) shot. After extensive patterning I have become convinced that the size four (4) is best in my particular gun.

You can easily kill a turkey with the standard shotgun using high powered shells or 2 3/4-inch magnum shells. I have killed lots of turkeys with an automatic shotgun equipped with a thirty-inch (30'') full choke barrel. I believe the magnum gun has caused a lot of turkey hunters to fail to kill his turkey simply because the turkey was out of the killing range of the gun.

A lot of changes have been made in guns and ammunition in the last few years. For any turkey hunter young or old I recommend he pattern his gun and the shells he intends using. Take several pieces of cardboard large enough to draw the outline of a turkey life-size. Try to draw the head and long neck as close to actual size as possible. Each cardboard and its turkey should be the same size and proportions. Place the cardboard at about the range you will shoot the turkey. Take a benchrest and try several different shells and shot sizes. Aim for a point on the turkey's neck midway between his head and the base of his neck. Your gun, fired at the proper range, should throw a circular pattern of shot. The top of the circle should hit the turkey in the head and the bottom of the circle should hit the base of his neck. The turkey's neck extends up through the circle, and hits should occur all along the neck. These are the most vulnerable areas of the whole turkey. Carefully count the shot placed in these vital areas by each shell and shot size. You can reach the simple conclusion from these tests as to which shell and shot size patterns are best in your gun. Several well-placed shots in these vital areas, at the proper range, will kill a turkey gobbler stone dead. Many footraces have been lost by turkey hunters in pursuit of a wounded turkey. It should be obvious at this point for you to realize that a shot aimed at the turkey's head would result in half of your pattern circle passing harmlessly over the turkey's head.

We assume you have already read this book. If you have and have carefully noted the advice of the old pro turkey hunters, you know how to make a turkey stand tall at the last second to enable you to squeeze off your shot at the fully extended neck and head of the turkey.

As I conclude my writing this book I want to make one final appeal to you to resolve to hunt this noble bird by fair rules. If you work at it, you can develop a large bag of tricks to put to your turkey. The possibilities of tactics and maneuvers are endless and the rules of fair play give you plenty of latitude to challenge your mind to come up with an idea which will help you bag your turkey. Every game has to be played by rules in order to establish the one who deserves to win. There will be no umpire or judge out there with you and the turkey to enforce the rules or law. This book has tried to help in establishing a code of ethics in turkey hunting. Abide by them.

Somewhere in this book it seems that I should mention the "luck factor in turkey hunting." In all my fifty-three years of hunting turkeys and talking with hundreds of other turkey hunters, I have concluded that luck doesn't have much to do with turkey hunting. You have to work hard to become a successful turkey hunter. That in itself adds to your enjoyment because any hardwon victory is for sure more appreciated.

I wish for every reader of my book a long and enjoyable turkey hunting career. I hope you will find some old gobblers, battle worn and wise, to challenge your expertise as a turkey hunter. Every time one of these old gobblers puts it on you, accept it. If he continues to win each encounter over a period of time, perhaps even years, appreciate it. Please stay with the rules as this turkey may demand of you the racking of your brain to invent some new trick to bring him to bag. If he does that, he has done you a favor. If he teaches you a lesson, that's desirable. If your turkey hunting career covers a long span of time, no doubt some old gobblers are going to survive in spite of your best efforts to bag them. Later in life as you meditate and enjoy the memories of your hunting years, up will come one of these old gobblers who bested you and finally at that point in time you will be the victor. Man, that's real turkey hunting.